Visual Arts Data Service

Creating Digital Resources for the Visual Arts

Visual Arts Data Service

Creating Digital Resources
for the Visual Arts:
Standards and Good Practice

Catherine Grout, Phill Purdy, Janine Rymer
(Visual Arts Data Service)
Karla Youngs, Jane Williams,
Alan Lock, Dan Brickley
(Technical Advisory Service for Images)

Produced by Oxbow Books for the Arts and Humanities Data Service

ISBN 1 84217 013 9
ISSN 1463–5194

A CIP record for this book is available from the British library

© Catherine Grout, Phill Purdy & Janine Rymer
(Visual Arts Data Service) & University of Bristol, 2000

Cover illustration © Visual Arts Data Service

This book is available direct from

Oxbow Books, Park End Place, Oxford OX1 1HN
(Phone: 01865–241249; Fax: 01865–794449)

and

The David Brown Book Company
PO Box 511, Oakville, CT 06779, USA
(Phone: 860–945–9329; Fax: 860–945–9468)

or from our website
www.oxbowbooks.com

Printed in Great Britain at
The Alden Press, Oxford

Contents

Section 1: Overview and Objectives

SECTION 1.1 THE AIMS OF THIS GUIDE AND OTHERS IN THE SERIES

This guide provides an introduction to and practical guidance on the issues involved in creating and developing digital resources for the visual arts.

Image-based resources are given primary focus as being the mainstay of visual arts applications, whilst recognised *standards and good practices* in data creation and management are indicated throughout, to promote the most effective production, usage and return on digital investment.

While there is an emphasis on information-based material, the guide also presents creative aspects and outcomes of working with digital resources in the visual arts. Practical exemplars will be referred to as much as possible.

In essence, the Guide aims to:

- Provide information and practical guidance concerning the issues involved in creating and developing digital resources.
- Introduce the possibilities offered by the creation of digital resources in the visual arts.

The Visual Arts Data Service, has produced this Guide in conjunction with the Technical Advisory Service for Images. VADS is also producing two other complementary Guides in this series:

- *Using Digital Information in Teaching and Learning in the Visual Arts* – is geared to the needs of both students and lecturers as well as practitioners in the visual arts and will focus explicitly on how digital resources can enhance, develop and inform the teaching and learning process. (With the CTI Centre for Art and Design.)
- *Creating and Using Virtual Reality: A Guide for the Arts and Humanities* – provides an introduction to the applications of virtual reality techniques for teaching, learning and research, with many current case studies of its use for the visual arts, performing arts and archaeology.

Where applicable, the guides are supplemented by case studies of current or recent projects. All guides contain appropriate glossaries of terms and bibliographies.

Although strictly a subject-based guide for the visual arts, the material herein and throughout the series should be of particular use to those in the wider cultural heritage field, as well as anyone interested in producing digital resources, particularly those involving images.

SECTION 1.2 THE GUIDE STRUCTURE AND HOW TO USE IT

What follows is an outline of the subjects and issues covered, followed by advice on how to use the guide.

The sections in this Guide

Section 1 Overview and Objectives – introduces the guide series and provides a brief introduction to digital resources in the visual arts.

Section 2 Copyright and Rights Management – provides advice about the main legal issues you are likely to encounter when creating and using digital resources. The reason that copyright and rights management issues are so intrinsic to this process is that if you translate something which already exists, be it a photograph, text, or work of art, into a digital format you are making a copy of it and therefore potentially breaching copyright. This section addresses:

- What the law states
- What constitutes the fair use of digital information
- The new issues created by electronic copyright and the Internet
- Advice about how to clear copyright for digitisation purposes

Section 3 Creating Digital Images – because much of the information at the fundament of the visual arts is by nature image based, a very common and useful digital resource will comprise a series of digital images of works of art, probably stored in some sort of database or other structure and accompanied by textual information to identify and contextualise them. Some of the chapters in this Guide therefore concentrate explicitly on the best way to go about creating, managing and preserving digital images. This Section draws upon the expertise developed by the Technical Advisory Service for Images (TASI) to provide advice on:

- How to select suitable equipment, hardware and software for digital imaging
- How to prepare image-based materials for digitisation
- How to create usable and good quality images which retain fidelity to their original sources.

Section 4 Standards for Data Documentation in the Visual Arts – the textual information which describes the works of art which exist in digital format is absolutely key. Over the years standards have emerged to help us logically group together pieces of information which we wish to use to describe works of art and to apply them consistently. These are supplemented by terminology standards and controlled vocabularies, such as the Union List of Artists Names and the Art and Architecture Thesaurus, which have a wide applicability within the visual arts and whose use can greatly enhance the usability and accessibility of the digital resources. Bad documentation can easily invalidate a good set of images which have been digitised with care. This Section provides:

- A survey of a set of established documentation standards
- Guidance about how to select appropriate documentation standards.
- A brief introduction to terminology standards and controlled vocabularies

Section 5 Project and Collections Management – this chapter concentrates on how to manage the whole process of creating a digital resource effectively. Particularly for larger scale initiatives, how well you manage the digitisation chain (for example, you may commence with items from a collection of analogue images of works of art and finish with a digital image database accessible and searchable via the Internet) will determine the success or failure of the whole project. This chapter recommends good practice concerning:

- How to choose a database or structure in which your images or other information are stored
- How to maintain workflow and check for errors
- How to manage the resources available for your digital resource creation process.

Section 6 Resource Delivery and User Issues – once you have created your resource you will face the issue of how to deliver it to its intended audience. It will be argued that the planning for this stage should happen as soon as possible in the life cycle of your resource creation project. An overview of resource delivery scenarios will be given here, including:

- Good practice in designing the way your digital resource is presented (its user interface)
- The standards which will allow the information in your resource to be exchanged with other information
- The support you may expect to provide to those who are using the digital resource you have created

Section 7 Storage and Preservation – the method that you use to store your digital resource is very important and without suitable storage you are in danger of losing your resource entirely through damage, obsolescence or inaccurate management of digital files. Any kind of loss of precious digital information is frustrating and is best avoided. This chapter gives advice on how to select and maintain sensible storage means for your digital resources. It also gives an introduction to digital preservation, which is a rapidly developing area. Since information stored in digital format has proliferated in a way we could never have predicted fifteen years ago, its long-term preservation and how to safeguard it against obsolescence and decay is fast becoming a global problem. This chapter introduces:

- Storage media for digital resources
- Practical steps that can be taken to tackle the preservation of vulnerable digital resources
- A number of projects and initiatives which address preservation issues

Section 8 Introducing Specialised Digital Formats to Create and Enhance Visual Arts Resources – this section of the Guide describes some of the most creative and innovative techniques that can be employed when creating visual arts resources. It looks at a range of techniques, some of which are now becoming more familiar and everyday, which offer many new vistas, both creative and information oriented, including:

- Web authoring and JAVA script
- Virtual reality
- CAD

- Multimedia
- Digital Animation

Section 9 Conclusion: From Creation to Deposit, Working with TASI and VADS – this section concludes by clarifying the services offered by the authors of this Guide, from all aspects of creating effective digital image resources to working with the Visual Arts Data Service to archive and preserve digital resources.

How to use this guide

As described above, the Guide is divided into nine chapters or sections including this one. Each of these sections is then divided into smaller subsections.

It is intended that each section can operate as a stand alone 'module'. Thus the guide does not necessarily have to be read in a linear order. However, if you are reading about this subject for the first time, we recommend you follow through the sections in order to gain most benefit. The issues involved in creating a digital resource are very much *inter-related* and the 'modular' structure of the guide reflects this. If you have prior knowledge of the subject, or have undertaken an initial reading, you may find it useful to employ the guide as a reference tool, and pick and choose areas of interest as needed.

Because we are attempting to provide guidance to those without any technical background or developed level of computer literacy we have deliberately tried to keep the language of the guide relatively free from technical jargon. Words which we do consider to be technical have been linked up to a Glossary which explains the meaning of the term the first time it appears in that subsection. We also hope that this Guide will be of use to those who have more experience of this area and we have therefore provided a Bibliography which points the way to more in-depth information about the subjects covered in the guide.

SECTION 1.3 INTRODUCING DIGITAL RESOURCES

A digital resource is in some respects the equivalent of its more conventional 'analogue' counterparts: the books, articles, reviews, library card indexes, or exhibition catalogues, upon which the whole process of research and teaching is dependent.

However the information which constitutes a digital resource is in machine readable format. This means it can be viewed and stored on a computer. If you were to view what was behind a section of an image of the Mona Lisa presented on the Internet for example, you would see something like this: "1001001010101010101101". This is the binary notation which defines the language that computers understand. This 'machine code' is the defining element of digital formats.

A digital resource, as this Guide will exemplify, could be a diverse number of things: a set of digital images of a work of art, a database, a digital video, or an environment created using virtual reality techniques. The following, existing singularly or in combination, could reasonably be described as a digital resource:

- An electronic text – e.g. the text in a word-processed document or on a web page
- A series of digital images – e.g. reproductions of works of art viewable on a computer screen

- A database – a collection of information ordered and entered in a logical way to create an electronic filing system that can be searched by the user
- A specialist piece of software – for example the programs on a personal computer that allow you to create and use digital information
- A virtual reality file – consisting of a visual environment which may be moved around giving the illusion of three-dimensional space

It may seem an obvious point to make, but the following would not constitute a digital resource as they cannot be stored or viewed on a computer: a mixed media installation; a building; a microfiche; a photograph; a card index; a vinyl record; a video tape. They are all analogue forms and can only be accommodated electronically by firstly 'capturing' them in a digital media.

Digital resources can be structured as per their more conventional counterparts. The information, for example, presented on a CD-ROM can look and behave very much like an exhibition catalogue, allowing the user to turn the pages of an 'electronic book'. However, digital media also allow us to transform our creative and research environments completely, into something which transcends the realm of direct information provision and becomes a creative work in its own right (for example, see Section 8.2 on using the Internet based language JAVA to explore Kandinsky's Figurines in a new way).

This Guide will primarily aim to provide pragmatic advice about how to go about the whole process of creating *information-based* image resources in digital format. However, we will also touch on the more exploratory aspects of this process where information provision becomes an act of artistic creation itself. For the purpose of this Guide, therefore, a digital resource is given a relatively broad definition: one that aims to accommodate the types of digitisation and engagement with digital techniques, which allow a range of new possibilities to be explored. The creation of all types of digital resources has exploded over recent years, along with the growth of networks and the provision of computing in research, education, artistic practice and the home. It is clear that in creating and using digital resources none of us leave the visual arts standing: digital resources develop, transform and enhance the Visual Arts and its study today.

SECTION 1.4 INTRODUCING STANDARDS AND GUIDELINES FOR DIGITAL RESOURCE CREATION

It is only by promoting and employing standards and guidelines in the way digital data is created, managed, stored and preserved that we can ensure its relevance to future generations and justify the sometimes heavy investments that are made in digitisation projects.

Since interest in digital media in the visual arts began, a great deal has been learnt about the best way to plan, implement and manage digital data creation. Pioneering projects have resulted in the evolution of 'good practices' and the fruits of all our labours in this area are therefore presented in this guide and the others in this series.

The creation of digital resources in the visual arts has previously followed an ad hoc path as regards methodologies for the production and management of digital projects. This can lead to incompatible resources of a short life span, even among those created in the same institutions, or by the same developers. This is a perfectly understandable situation in the light of new and evolving technologies and prior to the widespread use of networks and data sharing capabilities.

However, we are now at the stage where standards and guidelines are being constructed across experienced international communities. The application of these to digital resource projects greatly enhances the widespread use and long-term viability of projects, maximising the investments made in them and the potential digital technologies offer.

Standards and guidelines in the following areas are particularly addressed within this guide, as they can present the key to developing long-term and widely compatible resources successfully:

- Access issues
- Technical standards
- Documentation standards
- Preservation issues

1 Access issues

These include copyright, user needs and technical delivery issues. A resource which does not initially consider these may suffer from problems inhibiting the dissemination of the material, and would almost certainly need considerable work to make it function in situations where many users may wish to access the resource in a networked environment, e.g. over the Internet. Early attention to access issues, such as copyright, user needs and dissemination technology, will pay dividends for projects in the long term.

2 Technical standards

Using technical standards means that the common tools we use to create our digital resources, from hardware and software to the types of formats adopted, are less likely to become obsolete as technology develops. Using technical standards, such as the VADS/TASI preferred digital image formats (see Section 3.3), increases the lifespan of a resource, as we can predict with reasonable confidence that the digital environment chosen has a viable shelf life.

3 Documentation standards

These relate to how we structure and contextualise information. They are essential as on a basic level they are the things that allow us to share a common approach with others who are creating and using digital information, now and in the future. For example, if we have described digital images of works of art in a specified and established manner it is much more likely that our way of describing them will be understood by others and not only those who originally devised the resource and understand its structure. The application of documentation standards represents a universal rather than an idiosyncratic approach to data construction and as such enhances the use-value of a resource.

4 Preservation considerations

Archiving digital material has gained greater attention in recent years, as the need to preserve resources for the long term has become more apparent with accelerated developments in technologies and the raised awareness of the susceptibility of digital storage mediums to corruption. Digital preservation through correct storage, transferral and migration of data is now more highly regarded and it is reassuring that it is now becoming possible to decide upon how we can best safeguard the hardware, software and formats that are being used, so they will endure into the next decades. Archiving locally and/or with a service provider (see Section 9.2) is essential to ensure the long-term viability of data.

Conclusion

The promotion and application of standards and guidelines, along with collaboration between advisory services and resource creators, will help foster a common framework for creating and developing digital resources in the visual arts; a framework that utilises global standards whilst accommodating local situations, to the benefits of all.

The information provided in this guide will hopefully go some way to achieving that aim, by raising awareness of relevant issues and developments and promoting good practices.

Section 2: Copyright and Rights Management

2.1 INTRODUCING INTELLECTUAL PROPERTY RIGHTS (IPR)

This section looks at the very important issue of intellectual property rights (IPR) and focuses on *copyright*. This is both a *creation and access* issue. *It is paramount to address this concern as early as possible in the data creation process*, to ensure that you can firstly digitise material and secondly deliver the resultant resource you produce. This is why it is presented here first, not as an insurmountable obstacle, but as *a stepping stone to successful data creation*. Often perceived as a cause to panic, rights management is simply one link in the digitisation chain: with requisite knowledge, careful planning and thorough application it need be no more demanding than any other of the issues to be dealt with in undertaking digital resource creation.

There is no denying that IPR is a complex issue and this chapter firstly provides guidance by defining the relative aspects of IPR, in sections 2.1–2.6. This includes areas that are relevant to the resources created, as well as to clearing content for resource creation. Sections 2.7 and 2.8 discuss methods for handling IPR through documentation, such as Licences and User Agreements, for securing rights and defining usage of material. The final section, 2.9, posits strategies and methods for clearing IPR.

Introduction to copyright:

Copyright is the right to prevent third parties from copying (and doing certain other things) *without permission*. Failing to gain permission to copy materials is called 'infringement'; gaining permission is *good practice*. In the UK copyright is totally automatic, there is no need to register the work, pay fees or undergo any bureaucracy. Copyright is acquired when:

- The material is new (i.e. not copied).
- The material is in a fixed format.

1 New material

New material must be original, i.e. not a copy. If the material has been copied (e.g. a photocopy), the material is *not* granted copyright because this act of copying is an act of *infringement* of the original object's copyright. To gain copyright in some countries, new material must show some intellectual content but this does not apply to the UK.

2 Fixed format

The spoken word does not have copyright because it is not fixed. If, however, those words were recorded, they would then become fixed and would thus be subject to copyright. Likewise, copyright does *not* protect ideas, only the expression of those ideas. Digital materials do have copyright because they are fixed (and can thus be copied), and all material on the Internet is covered under copyright.

Copyright law

Copyright is a *property* right and is governed by law. The laws of copyright applicable to materials are initially those that exist in the country of origin of the material, but International Law also applies (see below). In the UK the most recent act was in 1988.

The Copyright Designs and Patents Act, 1988

This Act is the most recent revision of the copyright laws in the UK and came into effect in August 1989. It defines copyright materials by their medium and assigns life-spans to copyright (see Section 2.3).

International Copyright Law

The Berne Convention is currently the most important agreement covering International Copyright. It means that reciprocal treatment is given to a copyrighted work in virtually every country. The World Intellectual Property Organisation (WIPO) is addressing the different laws in different countries, including implications resulting from the growth of the Internet. Future European Law will also affect the copyright landscape in the UK.

Moral Rights

As well as Copyright, a creator also has Moral Rights attached to any materials created. Moral rights are different from copyright, but are just as important, and last for as long as copyright.
   Moral Rights are:

- The right to be identified as the author or creator (paternity right) – this applies to literary and artistic works
- The right to object to your name being attributed to something you did not create – this is to stop potential damage to your reputation. For example a tabloid newspaper may 'quote' from a person, but it is not actually a real quote. This is like libel.
- The right to object to derogatory treatment of your work – this is very important in digital imaging, where cropping, colour manipulation or adding features, are very easy processes in software packages.

Moral rights can *not* be assigned, even if the copyright has been, they remain with the creator. However the owner may wish to waive their moral rights and this feature is unique to UK Law. Moral rights do not apply to some types of materials, such as employee-created materials or journal articles. If a person wishes to copy a work it is important that they gain not only copyright clearance but also moral rights clearance as well.
   It should be noted, that it is only necessary to clear rights where material wanted for inclusion in a resource has its copyright held by a *third party*. If material is either in the 'public domain', or the resource creator is the rights holder, then there is no problem with including such materials within a digital resource.
   For specific advice on individual IPR issues, a consultation with a specialist lawyer is always recommended.

The remainder of this section investigates individual aspects of copyright in appropriate depth, and useful documentation for handling IPR, before addressing rights clearance strategies in section 2.9.

Disclaimer Notice

These sections do not constitute legal advice. They contain the interpretations of the copyright law by the authors. No responsibility will be taken for the interpretation of these sections by a third party. For specific advice on individual copyright issues, consultation with a specialist copyright lawyer is always recommended.

2.2 RESTRICTIONS AND PERMISSIONS: INFRINGEMENT AND FAIR DEALING

Copyright legislation has two main purposes:

- To encourage those who originate creative works to continue to do so, by enabling them to earn recognition/revenue from their efforts
- To offer protection to the creator/rights holder about how material can be used and represented

In so doing, copyright actually benefits resource creators in the visual arts! Firstly it protects creative activity, including that of digital resource production. Secondly, it encourages rights owners to introduce licensing schemes for their materials. The latter enables an effective strategy to manage third party rights clearing through the use of licences (see Section 2.7 for further information on licensing).

It is thus important to be aware of what are restricted and what are permitted acts regarding rights protected material, for both the inclusion of material and the use of a resource once created. 'Infringement' is a restricted practice and 'fair dealing' a permitted practice.

Infringement

An infringement of copyright occurs when a person carries out a restricted act *without permission*. Restricted acts are:

- copying material
- issuing copies to the public
- showing, playing or broadcasting or filming
- adapting or amending material

Only the copyright owner is legally allowed to perform the above or give permission for someone else to perform a restricted act. Thus *if you wish to do any of the above you must gain permission from the copyright owner*. This ensures protection of the commercial interests which belong to the copyright owner.

There are two types of infringement:

- direct infringement – when you are doing the infringing
- authorising infringement – this can range from a boss directly telling an employee to copy, or an organisation having a slack approach and thus no respect for the copyright law. This

negligence is the responsibility of the person right at the top of an organisation, e.g. Managing Director, Vice-chancellor. In Law, all are liable.

Direct infringement of copyright is both a civil and criminal offence. For an educational institution, most infringements will be a civil offence, i.e. no fines or imprisonment. This means that the copyright owner can sue for infringement of copyright through the courts. A claim could be made for [monetary] damages or for an injunction to be imposed. Where piracy of videos and CDs takes place, this is a criminal offence.

In the second type of infringement, i.e. authorising infringement, where an organisation has no regard for the copyright law, this may also be considered a criminal offence.

In order to infringe the copyright law, a person must have copied, etc., either the entire work or a 'substantial part' of the work. Substantial is not what one might think it is. For example, some think that copying 10% of a literary work is acceptable, as a substantial amount is not being copied. The test for substantial is to imagine that if the proposed material to be copied was missing from the original, would this cause considerable annoyance. If so, then it is considered to be substantial, i.e. it is the context or the quality that is the substantial part. An example would be copying the smile from the Mona Lisa.

As infringement is an offence, the infringer can be sued for financial implications to the original creator (i.e. loss of income), or for the profit that may have been made. It is an either/ or scenario. The person who infringed may also be liable to pay all court costs. The creator may arrange for an injunction to be issued stopping the person from using the material.

There are some defences against infringement of copyright, the most important of which is Fair Dealing.

Fair dealing

Fair Dealing is defined thus: 'an individual may make a single copy (or multiple copies in some cases) of all or a substantial part of a copyright item so long as it is "fair" and it is for one of the specified purposes'. Permitted purposes include:

- research or private study – not necessarily linked to a course. It can be any kind of research, including that for profit
- criticism or review – for example quoting from a book in a review of that book, with the review being published in a supplement of a Sunday paper
- reporting current events – can quote from a politician's speech as long as it is topical/ current.

It is important to note that in principle the copy can be hard, e.g. a photocopy, or an electronic copy.

So what is fair?

It is considered fair if it does *not* damage the legitimate commercial interests of the copyright owner. This can then raise the question of what is a legitimate commercial interest? For example, an image may be placed on a web site, and a researcher may use the image for his/her own research. The copyright owner may then sue, saying he was *planning* to develop the Web site and charge a fee for access to the images. The copyright owner may claim damages, and only has to prove that he was planning to commercialise the web site. What is fair can be difficult to judge, but obviously, multiple copying is worse than a single copy. Multiple copying will more likely affect a legitimate commercial interest.

Fair dealing can be a risky defence, and the person claiming fair dealing may lose in court. A lot of people who claim fair dealing are not actually infringing. Some questions to ask are: 'does it matter?', 'is the copyright owner going to find out?', and 'Will the copyright owner care?'. Some copyright owners choose to overlook infringements, which builds up into a 'custom and practice'. However a defence of 'custom and practice' may not stand up in court. Fair dealing applies as much to the electronic environment as to the print medium. Fair dealing is a defence against an infringement action, but the onus is on the defendant (the alleged infringer) to prove that the copying was for a permitted purpose and was fair.

Example of *fair dealing*: copying an article and putting it onto a floppy disk, for your own research or private study

Example of *non fair dealing*: copying an article, putting it onto a floppy disk, and then putting it onto a web site, i.e. electronically publishing infringed material.

The JISC and the Publishers Association have put together a report defining fair dealing. This is primarily concerned with literary works, but will also have an impact on images (digitised images are considered literary works). For images, there is no equivalent of the Publishers Association to look after the rights of images and the copyright owners. The joint report is available from:
http://www.ukoln.ac.uk/services/elib/papers/pa/clearance

Digital resource creation is unlikely to be an act of fair dealing as delivering the material will usually involve some form of 'issuing to a public'. Hence relying on a defence of fair dealing is not an alternative strategy to rights clearing.

2.3 DEFINING WORKS UNDER COPYRIGHT: CLASSIFICATIONS, TERMS AND OWNERSHIP

To determine if a work is in copyright and to gain permissions for its use, it is necessary to discover:

- The classification of work it falls under in copyright law
- The applicable terms, i.e. length of time that classification is granted copyright from its creation/publication date
- The rights owner

Copyright classifications

Copyright Law classifies works into different headings according to medium, and this is where the issue of copyright can become complex, as each classification has subtly different rules. The main classifications are:

- Literary works
- Musical works
- Dramatic works
- Artistic works (which includes images)

- Sound recordings
- Films
- TV broadcasts
- Others

Literary works is an important class and covers:

- All written works (hand-written, printed, published)
- Everything in machine readable digital form, including:
    digitised images
    everything on the Internet
    software

There is no implication of literary merit, but the work must be of a minimum length. This means that single words or a single sentence do not have copyright (for advertising – words, logos and sentences are 'trademarked'). Also individual facts do not get copyright, e.g. address details, telephone numbers. This is a common sense approach in that although individual facts do not acquire copyright, collections of such facts do acquire protection under the new Database law (see section 2.6).

Artistic works include:

- Graphic works
- Photographs (which have special rules attached to them)
- Sculptures
- Signatures
- Overhead Projector slides
- PowerPoint materials

As is the case for literary works, there is no implication of artistic merit. There is, however, some confusion about the status of works and which classification scheme they come under, and this is a really important issue that has to be understood. A photograph, for instance, is classified as an artistic work, but when this has been digitised (and thus becomes machine readable code), the digital image is then classified as a literary work. If this digital image is then printed out, it becomes an artistic work again. As there are different rules for artistic and literary classes, this can make copyright hard to keep track of.

Copyright terms:

Each classification for copyright has a *term* i.e. a fixed time span for which copyright will last. Once copyright expires, the work falls into the 'public domain' and can be used by anyone as they so wish.

For literary and artistic works, it is typically for 70 years from the end of the year that the creator died, when the creator is known. If the creator is anonymous, then the rule of 70 years applies from the end of the year the work was first published. There are, of course exceptions, such as: crown copyright, computer-generated work, published special editions, and photographs.

A subsequent amendment to the 1988 Copyright Act confused the issue of lifetime of copyright by acting retrospectively. This amendment came into effect on 1st January 1996. This meant that some materials that had come out of copyright suddenly gained copyright again. It increased the term of copyright (for some works) from 50 to 70 years from 31st December of the year the creator died. For anonymous works it is 70 years from the end of the year of original publication.

To determine if an item is in copyright it is best to refer to the law in operation at the time the material was created. For example if a poster design was produced in 1956, then you should refer to the 1956 Copyright Act to define the copyright owner and who to approach for clearance.

Copyright ownership:

As the Introduction 2.1 stated, there is no need to register a work for it to be protected by copyright. The consequence of this is that there is no national register or database in the UK where interested parties can research copyright ownership, although there are a number of useful organisations available (see Section 2.9).

As a guide, the *creator* is usually the copyright holder, unless the work has been carried out by an employee under a term of appointment, whereupon the *employing organisation* is usually the copyright holder.

This situation can be further confused if a subcontractor carries out the creative work. As freelancers are not an 'employee' they usually own the copyright. The onus is on the commissioner to negotiate rights when contracting freelance work. The commissioner needs to acquire a letter from the freelancer assigning the copyright to them. *Assignment of copyright must always be in writing.*

In the case of image work, particular care should be taken when subcontracting. For example, freelance photographers will not usually automatically assign copyright. Instead they will *license* the use of the commissioned photographs for a specific act(s). The freelancer thus retains the right to use the images for other purposes and also has the right to prevent unauthorised usage or to re-negotiate terms with the original commissioning party if other uses are desired.

It is always in the commissioners' interest to determine their immediate and long term needs and to negotiate any contract to make sure the requisite rights to materials are acquired, including the rights for electronic capture and dissemination, if that is the intention. (See Section 2.7 for more information on licencing.)

As copyright is a property right, ownership can change hands many times. It is important to remember this when trying to trace copyright ownership for work that you wish to use. Copyright can be sold, bought, given away or bequeathed in a will. This means that it can be difficult to know who owns the copyright at any particular time. The Act only tells you who owned the copyright at the creation of the work. It is also important to bear in mind that the present owner of an object, e.g. painting, or sculpture, may not be the copyright owner, as the object and copyright can be given, sold, bequeathed etc. separately.

Thus, one of the first steps in clearing copyright, will be to identify who is the current copyright owner for any material in question. (See Section 2.9.)

2.4 ARTISTIC WORKS AND COPYRIGHT

This class of copyright works obviously deserves further attention. This is doubly so as all materials in this class are also inherently *image forms* and are thus likely to be digitised for visual arts resources. Particular heed is paid to photographs as these often form the analogue source for digital image resources.

This class of works includes:

- Graphic works: e.g. paintings, drawings, models of buildings, diagrams, maps
- Engravings
- Autographs
- Photographs
- Sculpture
- Collage
- Overhead Projector slides
- PowerPoint presentations

As stated in Section 2.3, there is no implication of artistic merit. The creator is the owner of the copyright, unless it was created in the course of employment. Freelancers will also own the copyright unless they have assigned it in a written contract. Photographs are a problematic area as there are lots of different rules attached to them, for example if they are published or unpublished.

Photographs

If a photograph is of an existing artistic or literary work, then there are *two* copyrights, one copyright in the original object, and one in the photograph. Where multiple copyright exists in an item all copyrights must be cleared in order not to infringe each rights holder represented.

If the original item was in copyright at the time the photograph was taken, then the photograph is an infringement of copyright if permission was not granted. This may mean that you can own the copyright in a photograph but you can't do anything with the photograph because you are infringing the copyright of the original object.

If you want to take a photograph of an object in copyright, then you should apply for permission, stating with absolute clarity what you want to do with the photograph. This means that if the copyright owner grants permission they will be giving 'informed consent'. If you leave the details ambiguous and you exploit the photograph, that can be an infringement of copyright. Thus it is in your interest to keep the copyright owner fully informed of all details, including subsequent digital capture and dissemination if that is your aim.

Photographs have complex copyright lifetimes, depending on whether they are published (by the copyright owner) or unpublished. They are also subject to complex ownership rules.

Copyright terms of photographs

Unpublished photos have three different copyright lifetimes:

- 70 years from date of creation if made before 1.6.57
- 31st December 2050 if made between June 1957 and July 1989
- 70 years from date of death (if creator known) or of creation (if author unknown) if made since August 1989.

Published photographs also have complex copyright lifetimes:

- 70 years from date of publication if made before 31 July 1989
- As for unpublished if made since August 1989.

Ownership of copyright in photographic images

- If the photograph was made before 31st July 1989, it is either the person who commissioned the photo or the owner of the photographic film who owns the copyright. Proving ownership of the photographic film is especially difficult and very hard to prove.
- Since August 1989, copyright ownership is automatically placed with the photographer.

With photographs, it can be very difficult to ascertain who commissioned the photo, who owned the film or who the photographer was. In these circumstances it is best to make an intelligent guess, e.g. for a photo which is about 100 years old, it is safe to assume it is out of copyright. However, the onus is on the image user to find out if there is any copyright still attached to an old photograph.

Fair dealing and library privilege for photographs/artistic works

Fair dealing with photographs is generally the same as fair dealing with literary works. However, it cannot be done on photographs which are reporting current events.

There is *no* library privilege in artistic works either. Libraries are not allowed to make copies of artistic works for their patron. However, incidental copying of an artistic work whilst fulfilling a library privilege request on a literary work, can be permissible.

Photographing artistic works

Photographing an artistic work (or any other copyrighted work), without permission is an infringement of copyright, *unless the object is on permanent public display*, such as in a museum or gallery (whether for payment or not).

However, many art galleries and museums will not allow you to photograph an artistic work and they are perfectly entitled to impose their own rules. By entering a museum/gallery, you agree to abide by their rules. If you take a photograph when it is requested that you don't, you infringe on the rules of the museum/gallery, but *not* copyright.

Once copyright expires on an artistic work, as for any other category, it falls into the 'public domain' and can be used by anyone as they so wish.

Where multiple copyright exists in photographs, care should be taken to clear all relevant rights.

2.5 DATABASES AND COPYRIGHT

In the majority of cases a digital resource will result in a database of some sort, i.e. a coherent collection of data. Following a change in copyright law, on 1st January 1998, databases (electronic or non electronic) now have their own special rules. Databases can be granted copyright in themselves and/or a special 'database right'.

To classify a set of data as a database under copyright law a number of requirements have to be met:

- It is a collection of independent works that are literary works or data (i.e. facts), *including digital images*
- It is arranged in a systematic or methodical manner
- Each item is individually accessible by electronic or other means

Copyright for databases

For a database to gain full 'literary' copyright, it has to show *intellectual creation* in the selection or arrangement of its individual items. For example a conscious effort has to be made in including or excluding images, or in the application of metadata to the images.

Database right

If there is nothing intellectual or creative in the selection or structuring of a data collection it will get a special 'database right' instead.

Database right lasts for only 15 years, but it can be renewed. In effect, it can be renewed such that it lasts indefinitely (unlike copyright). Renewal can be achieved by showing that sufficient investment (whether by time and/or money) has been placed in the database such that additions, deletions or other amendments have been made during its last 15–year term.

Restricted acts against databases

- making copies
- making them available to the public

Permitted acts

- Adaptation and amendment

Fair dealing and databases

Fair dealing is allowed on a database, but *not* for commercial research (this is inconsistent with other literary works).

Combinations of rights for databases

- Each item in the database has full copyright *and* the database is creative, e.g. a newspaper. The database has double protection, i.e. from the copyright of the individual items and with copyright protection of the database as a whole.
- Each item has copyright, but the database is not creative, e.g. a collection of annual reports from all listed galleries in the UK. This work would only get the protection of 'database right'. The individual reports would get full copyright protection.
- Each item is non copyright, but the database is creative e.g. a set of phone numbers such as Yellow Pages. Copyright is given to the database as a whole, but the individual items are not protected by copyright.
- Each item is non copyright and the database is non creative, e.g. a residential telephone directory. This work would only get the 'database right' protection.

Generally for a database that contains digital images, skill and creativity will have taken place in deciding which images go into the collection and in structuring the metadata. Thus, digital image collections generally gain their own copyright, in addition to the copyright existent in any of their components.

2.6 ELECTRONIC MATERIAL AND COPYRIGHT

The nature of digital material and the philosophies of digital culture may sometimes lead to the disregard of IPR in this area. However this is not a good stance to take. IPR, as has been made clear, is applicable as much to the digital as to the analogue world and electronic material deserves as much, if not more, attention, due to misconceptions and IPR worries surrounding 'new media'.

Strictly speaking there is no such thing as 'electronic' copyright; it is a convenient term that is sometimes used to imply 'machine readable form'. Electronic copyright is *not* a legal or copyright term.

As revealed in Section 2.3, machine readable code is classified as a literary work and therefore the rules of literary classification apply to all digital materials, including digital images and models.

Moral rights and electronic material

Moral Rights also apply to digital material. It is thus important to acknowledge creators/rights holders, even if copyright has been assigned or licenced. Even in forwarding an e-mail message, the originator's name should be included, to comply with the right of paternity.

Copyright and the Internet

Copyright is extended to materials that are placed on the Internet. Internet material that is classified as literary works include:

- Web pages
- e-mail messages
- Software on ftp sites
- Compilations of URLs or e-mail addresses
- Search engines and web directories
- Frequently Asked Questions (FAQs)

Cases in law

The nature of the Internet and its relatively short history can mean that it is thought of as a grey area for copyright legislation, but Internet cases have arisen in law. These include: the Playboy magazine versus World Wide Encyclopaedia; Shetland Times versus Shetland News, and the TotalNews case.

Playboy magazine sued an Internet provider and won in the USA. This case proved that Internet Service Providers (ISPs) are liable for rights litigation, if they make a web service available and they know (or should have known) that a site was infringing copyright.

The Shetland Times vs. Shetland News case involved two rival newspapers and the use of hyperlinking to another site which objected. The case was settled out of court.

With the TotalNews case, copyright was infringed by taking material from other Web sites and putting it into a TotalNews frame, in a manner which made it appear they were the originators of the materials. This was not a copyright case but a US-based law of 'Passing Off', i.e. passing off the material as your own.

These cases show that care should be taken with hyperlinking, especially if re-disseminating information and making money from it. If you just give a URL, then there is no danger of copyright infringement. If, together with a URL, you provide a bit of information describing a site, make sure that it is an original and not copied description, unless written permission is gained to copy.

Digital material, including that on the Internet, is subject to IPR and should be treated with the same attention to rights management as all other forms of creative work.

2.7 HANDLING PERMISSIONS: PRO-FORMA AND LICENCES

To clear rights for the use of materials in a digital resource, *written* permission is required from the rights holder. This makes a *pro-forma* a particularly useful tool in rights management. A pro-forma is simply a standard document that can be sent to rights holders for their approval and signature. A rights clearing pro-forma should be drafted with the advice of a legal expert and provide for both parties' signatures: rights holder and resource representative.

The pro-forma should state clearly the *requisite permissions* required and include:

- The nature of the resource
- Exactly how the materials will be digitally captured and used
- Warranties and indemnities (see below)

It is often the case, particularly with images, that a rights holder will *not* assign full rights to a third party. Instead they will *licence* rights for particular purposes to a resource creator. A licence permits someone to copy or otherwise make use of material, whilst the rights owner retains and protects their rights to that material. Licences are thus a prime type of pro-forma for use in rights clearing for visual arts resources.

Licences

Licences should always be in writing, they represent a formal contract. Licences assume that all parties involved are equal. All licences should have a set of *terms* in the contract, to ensure that both sides are protected. Terms include:

1. Recitals and definitions
Including:

- who the parties involved are
- the resource description
- plans to distribute the resource
- definitions, such as: what is a digital image, what is downloading etc.

2. Copyright ownership
This should confirm:

- who the copyright owner is
- that *no* transfer of copyright ownership is written in the contract
- the wording appearing with each item e.g. © Visual Arts Data Service
- specific wording re use of the resource, e.g. 'you may not download'
- whether you can use each parties names in marketing

3. Restrictions on use
For example, that the distributor will endeavour to prevent illegal infringement, specifying categories of resource users, e.g. the public, or a student in the UK, Europe or the World.

4. Licence grant and royalties

- is it an exclusive or non-exclusive licence? Non-exclusive licences mean the rights holder retains the right to licence material to other parties, (this is the norm for Higher Education)
- whether for non-profit, or commercial arrangements concerning any incomes generated, and how this should be shared

5. Confidentiality
Including:

- is the owner entitled to the information about who is using the resource
- keeping the terms of reference of the contract confidential

6. Law
Which law is the contract governed by? This is very important because of the UK 'Unfair Contracts Act', which allows groups to get out of contracts where some clauses are unfair. The USA, for example, does not have this Act, which means that it would be very difficult to withdraw from a contract even though the terms are unfair.

7. Warranties and indemnities
This is a very important part of the licence – *it is essential that these should be obtained.* Business should *not* be done with a rights owner unless these are obtained. An Indemnity from the copyright owner will state that the item(s) and associated metadata used do not infringe any other persons or groups, copyright or any other laws. This will absolve the resources liability, if such infringements subsequently come to light. However if the images or metadata are changed without the express permission of the copyright owner, then the warranty becomes void.

8. Data handling
This states exactly what can be done to the materials in their digital form.

9. Marketing
This sets out the marketing strategy and states what can be used for testing, training and demonstrating the service.

10. Length of agreement
This can specify a fixed time period or leave to run indefinitely.

11. Arbitration
This sets out means of arbitration of a dispute should the two parties fail to reach an agreement.

12. Termination
This will define how either party can terminate the agreement, e.g. by failing to meet their duties of the contract. Clauses can be specified, where if one party fails to deliver, the other party can claim compensation.

13. Force Majeure
This states that if forces beyond control result in one group failing to deliver their services, then the contract cannot be terminated.

Licences may appear complicated but they are necessary legal documents that ensure all parties are clear and in agreement on the rights situation surrounding a resource and its components. When drafting a licence for digital media it is important to make sure that all long-term as well as short-term eventualities are covered. Consultation with a legal expert and advisory bodies for resource creation is strongly advised.

2.8 USER AGREEMENTS

User agreements define what *users* of a resource can and cannot do with the material in a resource, particularly regarding copyright. They also stipulate the obligations and rights of the resource creators/rights holders.

Where a resource includes material granted by third party rights holders, user agreements form an essential role in rights management and negotiation. They not only inform users as to permissible acts regarding a resource and its components, but also act as a guarantee that infringement of third party rights is being guarded against.

Depending on the degree of protection required, user agreements can vary in their formality, from a 'notice' on a resource stating something such as: 'in using this material users are agreeing to abide by [particular rules and regulations], including the laws of copyright', to formal contracts that have to be submitted by users, either on-line or on paper.

User agreements will depend on the rights situation regarding material used. If third party rights holders have given permission for inclusion of their materials, permitted usage will have been negotiated into the agreement between rights holder and resource creators. For example: 'for viewing only', 'downloadable' 'for single use' etc. If material was rights free, or the resource creators owned the rights, it is they who can stipulate conditions.

In all cases, copyright will apply to a resource and/or its components, unless copyright is either out of term, or explicitly waived. Thus it is always important to make users aware of the rights situation governing material available.

This subsection sets out the legal nature of user agreements and suggests issues to be included in them. (See Section 6 for further discussion of User Issues.)

User agreements

User agreements form a type of contract in which the parties involved do not have equal status. One group (the rights holders), will be imposing terms on another (the users/clients). This places such agreements under 'Unfair Contract Terms'. These state that:

- All terms must be reasonable
- There must be a choice of Law under which the contract is made

Issues to include

The following should be included in user agreements to protect the rights of resource creators/ rights holders and to make users aware of their obligations.

- The right to change data available, at short notice (including changes to costs if it is a commercial resource – with the proviso of reasonable notice and the option for the client to withdraw if they do not like the new charges).
- The resource distributor's obligations regarding notification of any changes
- The means of specifying rights terms, e.g. lettering on images, rights statements etc.
- Specification of limits of use, i.e. what the user can and cannot do with a digital image or other item.
- Observation of security issues, including confidentiality of any password allocated
- The right to terminate the user agreement on the part of the resource administrator if users abuse the system

Whatever form a user agreement takes, whether an informal notification or formal submitted document, it is recommended to gain legal advice when drafting their content.

2.9 CLEARING RIGHTS

Obviously, if material is either out of copyright, or the resource creator is the rights holder, then there is no problem with a material's use within a digital resource. Rights clearance is only required where a material's copyright is held by a third party.

There are three initial steps in clearing rights for use of materials in digital resources:

- Identify materials requiring third party rights clearance
- Identify rights holders of those materials
- Contact and request the written permissions required to digitise and utilise those materials. This is best achieved via a pro-forma or licence agreement

This section deals with the principles and procedures involved in following these steps. (See Section 2.7 for an in-depth look at drafting a pro forma, especially licence agreements.)

There are a number of scenarios that can occur when clearing rights, depending on whether rights details are known or unknown. However, the most important thing to do is to *document* all efforts. A *diligence file* should be kept of all measures taken, all communications sent, and any replies (both positive and negative). This is not only a good administrative strategy, but also reduces any risk of purposeful or negligent infringement. Diligence files prove that 'best endeavours' have been made to clear material for digital usage.

Clearance scenarios

- Rights details known
- Rights details initially unknown:

1. Rights details known
Action: contact and gain requisite permissions:

- Request permission for digitisation and usage of copyright materials – be very clear about:
    the nature of the resource materials are to be included in
    the uses that will be made of materials
    how long materials are to be used for, e.g. in perpetuity
    restrictions on the users of the resource
- Send a *pro forma* including an indemnity clause for the copyright owner to sign and return (see Section 2.7).

Possible outcomes

- Permission not granted – in this situation *do not* even think of digitising
- Rights holder wishes to think about it and get back – this in effect means *no* until permission is given
- No response at all – this is a *no*, do not assume silence is unspoken consent – keep trying
- Yes, agreement signed and returned – you can go ahead and digitise

The rights owner is quite within their right to ask for a fee for use of their material and/or specify conditions, such as rights statements or access restrictions to apply to their materials usage. Usage may then become a matter of further negotiation and specialised agreements may have to be drawn up. If a fee is thought too large, appeal can be made to the Copyright Tribunal.

2. Rights details initially unknown:
Action: Identify and contact rights holder:

- begin from the assumption that the rights holder is either:
    The individual creator
    The organisational creator/employer of creator
    The commissioned freelancer
    other, e.g. rights beneficiary
- Use tools such as directories of artists and works, in combination with telephone directories etc.
- Contact a relevant organisation, e.g. ALCS (Authors' Licensing and Collecting Society) for authors, Copywatch at the University of Reading, and the Copyright Licensing Agency, to see if they can help
- As a last resort, advertise or place a letter in a trade journal or national newspaper asking for relevant information

Possible outcomes:

- The rights owner comes forward – follow the actions above for gaining written permission.
- There is no forthcoming information and the creator or rights holder is unidentifiable – in this scenario it is a matter of risk assessment for the resource producers. If you choose to go ahead and digitise, the rights owner may come forward after digitisation. In such a case, they are still within their rights to claim compensation, recognition and/or withdrawal of the digital copy. If a digital image is used in this situation, *flag it* with a notice stating how 'best endeavours were made to clear copyright...' This supplements the diligence files to prove that best endeavours and intentions were made and any subsequent negotiations can proceed from there.

Good practice for Rights Management

If in doubt about a specific individual rights matter, consult a legal IPR expert.

- Tackle the complexities of rights management *early* on in your project and define procedures to do so.
- Assign special responsibility for rights management to a member of the resource team and make all staff aware of the issues involved.
- Make sure all agreements regarding copyright and associated rights are *in writing*, and keep them for the *lifetime of the project.*
- Use pro forma *licences* and *user agreements* to handle and document rights management.
- Make provision for *moral rights clearance* as well as copyright.
- Where *multiple copyright* exists in an item, such as a photograph or film/video *clear rights from each rights holder* represented.
- Gain permission to move and change formats *in perpetuity*, so that permission does not have to be sought every time the image is 'migrated' through media and file formats.
- Make rights information part of the *metadata* accompanying digital items.
- Negotiate permission with digital preservation in mind. If possible, gain permission to deposit and make material available via an on-line archive.

Section 3: Creating Digital Images

3.1 INTRODUCING DIGITAL IMAGES AND IMAGE CREATION

Digital images are likely to form an integral part of any digital resource created for the visual arts.

Creating digital images, also known as 'image capture' or 'image digitisation' or 'image acquisition' is a specialised technological area in terms of hardware, software and skills required. This section aims to provide:

- sufficient information for those who wish to carry out digital image creation themselves
- the 'background' knowledge necessary for those who may 'out-source' image creation, recruit specialised staff and/or buy-in technology.

This is achieved by looking at the following:

- Digital images as objects in themselves: defining their component structures and reviewing the file formats available, to induce an understanding of the media (Sections 3.2 – 3.3).
- The technologies for image capture, including scanners, digital cameras and relevant software.
- The production processes involved, including good practice recommendations.

Introducing digital images

A digital image is simply another form of representation. It has its own vagaries and nuances as much as a painting, photograph or sculpture etc. It just happens to involve and rely upon computer technology. As a medium, digital imaging has its advantages, disadvantages, proponents and sceptics and, as with all media, creating digital images is learnable, controllable, manageable and can be rewarding.

The guide will concentrate on digital image creation for primarily information-based resources, rather than as an artistic end in itself, and hence focuses on creating high quality 'photo-realistic' digital images, suitable for archiving. These principles are directly transferable and highly recommended for image creation for purely 'artistic' ends.

Introducing digital image creation technology

The means of creating a digital image relies on turning light into electrical signals, which can then be reinterpreted into a visual image, either on a computer screen or in print. The technology that is chiefly employed to do this task is called a Charged Couple Device (CCD). CCDs form the essential capture component in the majority of digital imaging equipment.

The most prominent capture devices are scanners and digital cameras. They essentially perform the same types of function, but are packaged for varying needs.

Scanners and digital cameras are discussed more fully in sections 3.5 and 3.6 respectively.

Introducing the production processes

Creating high quality digital images suitable for information and archiving purposes essentially involves two interrelated processes.

- Primary image capture/acquisition, consisting of the following stages:
  Pre-digitisation feasibility study
  Digitisation
  Post-digitisation processes
- Manipulation for specific purposes, including:
  archiving
  electronic publishing
  network-delivery
  portable-storage
  print publishing

Given the necessary technology, understanding and skill, digital images are easily manipulated. Primary acquisition can result in a digital image file from which surrogates for varying purposes can be produced.

The primary acquisition process thus becomes the key to producing high quality images suitable for all subsequent image needs. It is far better to capture once for all purposes than several times for each purpose. (Section 3.7 discusses the image-digitisation process in finer detail.)

3.2 DIGITAL IMAGES

When discussing digital images it is important to remember that they can be manipulated, and that from a single 'master digital image' varying needs can be satisfied through creating 'surrogate' (varying copies of) images in imaging software. That area will be discussed in later sections. This section looks purely at the nature of digital images.

Types of digital images
Computer graphics come in two main types:

- Vector based – geometric
- Raster (also known as bit-mapped) – photo-realistic

Vector based images
Vector based images consist of a series of geometrical objects: lines, ellipses, polygons etc. Each of these objects will have a number of properties associated with it: for example, position, line thickness, line colour, line style and so on. These properties can be considered as a series

of instructions that are 'played back' by the drawing engine to reconstruct the image on the output device.

Typical examples of vector based images are technical illustrations, floor plans, maps, diagrams and charts. Vector based images are commonly used in Computer Aided Design (CAD) and drawing software. The advantages of these formats are that:

- objects remain independently editable
- file size is relatively small
- images can be scaled or resized without loss of resolution

Raster/Bitmapped images

Raster/Bit-mapped images are made up of a mosaic of picture elements, called *pixels*. Pixels are the familiar square features seen when a digital image is zoomed into. Each pixel contains the colour information about that point of the image and the combination of pixels constructs the entire image.

Raster image file sizes tend to be large, because of the amount of information each pixel holds and the number of pixels necessary to make a high fidelity image. The main advantages of raster formats are:

- high degree of photo-realism obtainable
- high degree of manipulation possible, as each pixel can be edited on an individual basis

A third class of digital image file, known as *metafiles*, refers to formats that can contain both vector and bit-mapped information, either together or separately. An example would be an architectural CAD package that allows photo-realistic images to be rendered onto a vector structure to add realism to computer models.

The focus throughout this section is totally upon raster type images, because it is photo-realistic images which are highly prominent in information-based resources in the visual arts. Unless otherwise stated, the term 'digital image' will from here on refer to a bitmapped/raster type image.

Defining features of digital images

There are five main defining elements to a raster/bitmapped image:

- File size
- File format – how the image is structured
- Resolution – number of pixels or pixels per unit length
- Bit depth – amount of information in each pixel
- Colour space – colour the image is in e.g. RGB, CMYK

File size

A digital image, as was made clear in Section 2.1, is ultimately based on machine readable code. The first defining element of any digital image is thus its *file size*, the amount of computer-code information within it. As with all computer file-sizes, it is expressed in bytes and usually in factors of approximately 1000, (actually 1024, as computers use binary, not decimal system):

- 1 kilobyte (KB) = c1000 bytes
- 1 megabyte (MB) = c1000 kilobytes (a million bytes)
- 1 gigabyte (GB) = c1000 megabytes
- 1 terabyte (TB) = c1000 gigabytes

The file-size is important as it affects:

- quality of image
- storage space requirements
- network delivery speeds.

In general, the larger the file size the higher the quality of the image, the greater the storage requirements and the slower the network delivery speeds possible.

It is likely that 'master', 'archival' images and those required for high quality print-publishing or conservation analysis will have large file sizes, usually in the megabytes or even giga or terabytes. Those for network delivery are likely to be in kilobytes or less.

NB: A drop in file-size, does not necessarily mean a disastrous or even perceivable loss in visual information, as there are special 'compression formats' whose purpose is to reduce file sizes, whilst maintaining optimum visual information. These are discussed further below.

The remaining four defining elements of digital images all affect file-size.

File formats

File formats relate to the type of computer coding that is used to structure a digital image. File formats have grown from varying developers and fulfil differing needs for an image: from large file-size, high quality print publication, e.g. TIFFs, to low file-size screen resolution 'thumbnails', e.g. GIF. Each have their advantages for various functions and it is possible to transfer a digital image between file formats, (See section 3.3 and 3.4.).

Resolution

Resolution is the number of pixels in a digital image. It is commonly given as a the number of pixels per unit length, expressed as 'ppi' (pixels per inch) or dpi (dots per inch – a term inherited from printing). The higher the resolution, the higher the quality of image and possible output size.

Bit depth

This is the amount of colour information per pixel in an image. It is often measured in factors of 8, i.e. 8bit, 16bit, 24bit, 32bit etc. – there are 8 bits to a byte, (some formats, e.g. .GIF can can use other than 8 bits per pixel). 256 colour images have 1 byte (8bits) per pixel and 'true-colour', (16.7million colour), images have 3bytes (24bits) per pixel – 1 byte per 'red', 'green' and 'blue'.

Colour space

The colour space a digital image is in relates to its achievable colour output. There are two prominent types:

- RGB
- CMYK

RGB
This is an additive colour process, using Red, Green and Blue, which is commonly used by computer monitors to display digital images.

CMYK
This is the colour space used for the print industry. It is a 4–process colour system using Cyan, Magenta, Yellow and Black.

(Transferring between colour spaces will not necessarily result in accurate colour rendition, hence the importance of 'colour management systems' in image capture, see Section 3.7.)

File compression

Compression is one way of reducing file size. It is achieved by transferring the image-file into a format which uses specially created algorithms (mathematical formulae), to reduce image file sizes logically. There are two types of compression:

- lossless
- lossy

Lossless compression

This uses mathematical processes that, typically, encode repeating elements within an image. For example, stretches of pixels that share the same colour are taken and stored in just two bytes; one for colour and the other for the number of adjacent pixels.

This type of compression is designed to ensure no loss to visual perception of the image. Additionally, a compressed file of this type can be decompressed, and the image restored to exactly as it was prior to compression, hence 'lossless'.

Compression ratios are not very high, typically reducing file sizes by a half.

Lossy compression

These techniques are capable of much higher compression ratios, sometimes in excess of 100:1. The price to be paid for this is a reduction in image quality; the file after compression is not the same as that before compression, as data have been removed. The degree of image degradation depends on the image content and the amount of compression applied. (See Section 3.3 for examples of each type of compression format.)

Colour-space changes and compression

Reducing colour space is a form of 'lossy' compression, e.g. reducing a 24bit (16.7 million) colour image to 8bit (256) colour means the lost colour information cannot be restored. The file size reduction in this case would be 3:1, without further compression techniques.

Lossy compressed image file formats should not be used as a 'master' or 'archival' format, but they are ideal for surrogate images intended for electronic delivery.

3.3 SELECTING IMAGE FILE FORMATS

The file format chosen depends, in part, on:

- The nature of the object/event being captured
- Intended use of image/stage in creation process

Nature of the object/event

The nature of the object/event being captured may well affect the choice of file format, e.g. in the case of digitising greyscale images such as black and white, or tinted prints, using a 24bit (full-colour) format would be unnecessary. Similarly, when capturing a real-time event with a digital camera, format choice could be constrained by the camera specifications. (See Section 3.6.)

Image end-use/creation stage

The intended use of an image, i.e. its stage in the production process, will have a profound affect on file formats chosen. These are discussed more fully below in relation to:

- Primary acquisition
- Manipulation
- Archiving
- Delivery surrogates

Whatever the stage, formats chosen for images to be used in information-based resources should minimise, or at least postpone for as long as possible, any data loss.

Primary acquisition

This is the first and most important step in the process. The primary acquisition file format should:

- Be lossless so as to maintain the highest possible fidelity to the original object.
- Retain the best colour/greyscale information possible – at least 24bit colour/8bit grey
- Retain any acquisition device gamma/colour calibration information

Suggested primary acquisition formats: TIFF; PNG; SPIFF
PNG and SPIFF meet a lot of the requirements for a modern raster image format; amongst other features both:

- Are open non-proprietary formats
- Support metadata as text (some fields predefined)
- Support lossless compression (SPIFF supports lossy as well)

At the time of writing support for PNG is patchy but increasing, SPIFF has yet to 'take off' but most JFIF readers (i.e. most JPEG software) should be able to import the file. Until support for both these formats increases, TIFF is probably the 'safer' format – consider migrating files as support increases.

Manipulation/editing (working within imaging software)

Image manipulation/editing software should read and be able to edit standard image formats. However, if a *substantial amount* of editing is required on any individual image then proprietary formats of graphics programs, e.g. Photoshop .psd, can be very useful. These proprietary formats offer functionality not available for use with standard formats.

Temporarily changing or copying files to proprietary formats within imaging software means extra information specific to editing can be held. This allows manipulation to be saved and continued between editing sessions.

If proprietary formats are used for editing, then once final editing has been reached for an 'archival master' or 'delivery image', the edited image file should be saved or copied into the appropriate, non-proprietary format.

Archiving

The 'archival master' should be at the highest practicable resolution, in keeping with the storage facilities available (preferably as per acquisition resolution and format). With mass storage becoming less costly all the time and with more types to choose from (e.g. CD-ROM; DAT tape; DVD; removable disks i.e. JAZ and ZIP; optical discs), there are options to suit most budgets (for a fuller discussion of storage media see Section 7).

The archival format should:

- Be lossless so as to maintain the highest fidelity
- Retain the best colour/greyscale information possible – at least 24bit colour/8bit grey
- Be a standard format readable by most image editors/viewers
- Preferably hold metadata associated with the image. e.g. cataloguing, copyright information – the data will then move with the image, making retrieval easier and lost or broken databases less problematic

Suggested archival formats: TIFF; PNG; SPIFF

When archiving considerations are paramount or digital images are being used as a method of preservation of original objects, it may be appropriate to maintain both a copy of the 'primary acquisition' file and the 'archival-master'. In effect, two types of 'archived' image are kept: an *'archival-original'* (unedited primary acquisition file) and an *'archival-master'* (edited primary acquisition file).

Delivery

Delivery formats are dependent upon end-user needs and the dissemination technologies involved. There are numerous factors to consider, including:

- Type of destination device, i.e. the end-needs of the users, e.g. on-screen, print, slide
- The capabilities of the receiving device(s) – colour capabilities, resolution and formats supported
- Delivery medium – networked or portable storage device
- Image use after electronic delivery – print output etc.
- The nature of the image, e.g. photo-realistic or presentation

One distinction to make is between that of delivery for:

- print publication
- electronic publication

Suggested print publishing formats

Consult with those doing the printing: this becomes even more important if it is a commercial printer. Commercial printers often want something along the lines of a TIFF/EPS file in CMYK format and it may be necessary to have a printer profile.

On-line delivery formats:

- Where bandwidth or storage space are a problem, then consider JPEG (at least for preview files), PNG (8bit) or GIF. For JPEG the degree of compression used will depend on the amount of acceptable degradation

In the future an appropriate use of technology may enable duplicates of the 'archival-master' file to be delivered by performing an 'on-the-fly' conversion to deliver a file that is in the resolution, colour depth and format that end-users require.

For non-networked electronic publishing:

- If bandwidth is not an issue then consider using TIFF or PNG (24/48bit)
- For electronic presentation-type images the choice is generally simpler – use PNG (8bit) or GIF

If SPIFF support becomes more widespread then it can be used for photo-realistic and presentation types of image under most conditions.

Screen display:

It is also worth noting that the type of monitor which a digital image is viewed on will affect the way it appears. Differences in monitors which can affect screen display include:

- Screen gamma values
- Monitor set up, i.e. position, brightness, contrast, colour temperature etc.
- Type of screen: VDU, TFT panel or projection system?
- Colour depth and resolution e.g. 256 colour or 'true-colour'

It is most important when deciding upon delivery formats to choose the ones that best suit the circumstances of the end-user.

Suggested formats for image creation for high quality information-based resources is summarised as follows

Purpose	Format
'Primary acquisition' image	TIFF (24bit) minimum with thumbnail enabled
'Master/archival' image	TIFF (24bit) minimum
Networked electronic delivery	JPG, PNG (8bit) or GIF
CD ROM/DVD publication	Dependent on number of images and requirements of subject matter, anything between 'Master/archival' image format and 'network delivery' format.
Print publishing	Check with publishers requirements

Table 1: TASI/VADS suggested formats*

*These are as at the date of publication. As noted above, the file format scene is a continually advancing one and recommendations are subject to change. Please check the web-version of this guide for latest recommendations, or contact TASI/VADS directly. These suggestions are a guide, not gospel; individual image creation projects may well have idiosyncracies that are better suited to other formats. If necessary, contact a digital image consultancy to discuss individual needs. (Appendix 1 carries a list of useful organisations.)

3.4 IMAGE MANIPULATION AND IMAGING SOFTWARE

Introduction

When creating digital images for information-based resources, it will often be the case that as close an adherence to the original object, be it a 'real' physical object or photographic representation etc., will be desired at all stages of image creation. This is called maintaining fidelity with the original. However, it will usually be the case that some degree of *'image manipulation'* will be needed after 'primary acquisition', both to create a 'digital master/ archival image' and to create any subsequent surrogate images for delivery needs.

Image manipulation refers to working with or 'editing' digital images. Digital images can be altered in all their dimensions, including transfer between varying file formats.

Some common image manipulation tasks are:

1. Reorienting images – to landscape/portrait etc.
2. Cropping – taking out borders etc. if necessary
3. Cleaning images – removing post-capture irregularities, dust etc.
4. Adjustment of :
    - colour
    - brightness
    - contrast
5. Re-sizing – if necessary
6. Reformatting/compressing – for various needs, delivery etc.

One to four are likely to occur when creating a 'master/archival' image from the 'primary acquisition' image, (although all should be optimised at capture), and five and six when creating surrogate delivery images from the 'master/archival image'.

Image manipulation is *not* a 'something for nothing' process or a 'cure all'. It will always be a case of balancing various needs. All changes will alter a 'digital image file' and the following aspects – size, resolution and bit-depth – cannot be increased after initial capture without degradation. They are effectively set at their maximum at the capture stage, hence the need for the 'primary acquisition' image to cater for all planned uses.

Imaging and manipulation work requires good vision, particularly colour-vision. It is important to be aware that not everyone possess full colour vision.

Determining manipulation needs

The degree of manipulation will depend upon:

- The quality of the 'primary acquisition' image
- The purpose of manipulation, whether it is to produce a 'master/archival' image or a surrogate for delivery/other purposes.

Primary acquisition image quality

Obviously if the 'primary acquisition' image is of a high quality, there may be no or very little need for any manipulation. If, however, for unavoidable circumstances the object captured is of poor visual quality, e.g. a discoloured photograph, there may be a need for manipulation to achieve a desirable image. (That is, providing the actual condition of the photograph is not the object of the digitisation exercise; see 'Defining the prime informational content of the capture image' below for further discussion).

Manipulation is a skilled process and can take significant time and costs, so this highlights the importance of 'pre-acquisition assessment'/feasibility studies of objects to be digitised, as well as high quality capture procedures, see Section 3.7.

Manipulation purpose: manipulating for a 'master/archival' image

Two considerations here are:

- Defining the prime informational content of the captured item
- The importance of fidelity to the original captured object vs the importance of a 'visually good' image

Defining the prime informational content of the capture image

This relates to whether the aim of capture is fidelity to the slide or photo itself, or the content represented within it. For example, a slide in an art historian's collection of an architecturally important building has the building as the informational focus rather than the slide itself. It would be more important to maintain fidelity with the actual building rather than how the slide represents it. Of course, in an ideal situation, there will not be a discrepancy between a slide, or other image representation, and the content it represents, but this is not always the case, as a result of the ravages of time and use etc. One advantage of digital image capture is that any such 'degradation' on the 'original' image can be alleviated.

Ultimately the state of the original image-object and the quality of the 'primary acquisition' process will determine the amount of manipulation required in this scenario.

Fidelity to original versus 'visually pleasing' image

Most of the time this will be one and the same thing and should require little or no manipulation, providing both the original to digitise and the primary acquisition process have been quality controlled.

An example of a case when it may not be the same thing arises when capturing for conservation or preservation analysis, where the existent 'visual flaws' are precisely the object of scrutiny. This is really a question of defining which part of the image-content is of prime importance (as above), and of course the beauty of digital imaging is that a 'cleaned-up' image can also be produced for comparison etc.

Another situation where this balance may need to be assessed more thoroughly is where the end-needs can be precisely determined as being for 'visual-promotion' only. In this scenario, visual appearance could outweigh fidelity to the 'primary capture' object. If this is the case, manipulation from 'primary acquisition image to 'master/archival' image could be more demanding. (In such a situation, it would be of even greater importance to maintain the 'primary acquisition' image as a 'fallback' archival image.)

Manipulation purpose: manipulating for a surrogate delivery image

Manipulation at this stage should occur from the 'master/archival' image, which has already had any necessary 'post-acquisition' manipulation done.

Manipulation carried out at this stage will change the file-size considerably. However, in terms of manipulation processes, it is likely to be simpler as it will only involve re-sizing and reformatting the image into a suitable type for networked delivery, unlike the more complex process of adjusting colour etc. An example of this is the common processes of turning large high resolution 'TIFFs' into smaller web-deliverable 'GIFs'.

The better imaging applications will come with built-in batch processing, enabling manipulation procedures to be automated for high volumes of image. For example re-sizing and reformatting, to the same degree for each image, can be achieved using these methods.

Imaging software

In order to manipulate a digital image, *'Imaging'* software is required. Common types include 'Adobe Photoshop' (http://www.adobe.com/prodindex/Photoshop/main.html), and 'JASC Paintshop Pro' (http://w.jasc.com/psp5.html). This section discusses the various issues involved in assessing imaging software for resource creation needs. Further details on individual imaging software packages are available from: http://www.tasi.ac.uk/building/image_cap1.html

Issues in choosing image software applications

There is a wide selection of image handling software currently available with varying facilities. The cost of software ranges from nothing (freeware) to several thousands of pounds, for 'industry standard' packages.

The following factors should be considered when selecting imaging software:

- Cost
  This is not only for purchasing the application, but should also cover training and familiarisation for proposed users as necessary

- Hard disk space
  Allow space not only for the program but also for its working files, work-in-progress and the almost inevitable accumulation of images. Some applications have large hard disc requirements when working in certain modes designed for handling large images.
- Processor power/speed
  Complex operations, especially sequences of them, on large images can soak up processor power all too easily
- Memory
  Most applications need available RAM of 2–3 times the uncompressed image size. This is for the image, undo information and working space. More complex operations will tend to increase the amount of RAM required.
- Graphics card/Display capability
  A 16.7M (24bit) display card for anything other than casual image work should be the minimum standard. 64K (16bit) are usable for some work (depending on image type) but 256 colour (8bit) displays are not suitable for working on images.
  Most current graphics adapters offer a reasonable degree of display acceleration – as usual more speed generally means higher cost. Make sure that the card you have has enough memory (or is upgradeable) to run your monitor at its highest usable resolution in 24bit colour.
- Monitors
  17" is a good starting point, larger if you have the money/desk space. Always match the display card capabilities and set the monitor up properly (refer to hardware and software manuals for information on how to do this).
- Software
  Ensure the application is compatible with the operating system in use. Check for cross-platform operation, if this is important and if the software is an add-on to another program check the requirements of the the other program.

All applications should come with a specification for hardware and software requirements. Check these against any hardware and software in place or to be bought. It is advisable to work to suppliers 'recommended requirements', rather than 'minimum requirements'. (The latter may allow the program to run, but working speed may be inadequate.)

Imaging software requirements checklist

Essential features checklist

- Import and export facilities for the file formats to be used
- Support of the required features of those formats, e.g. metadata
- Ability to manage the size of images you require
- Ability to have more than one image open at a time
- Ability to handle the range of operations normally needed
- Adequate handling of the operations you will use only occasionally or add-ons available to do so
- Ability to save workspace settings for work in progress, so that work can pick up where it was left off
- Colour management support

Useful features checklist

- Calibration support, for monitor/printer etc.
- Multi undo levels
- Batch/macro facilities for volume/repeat operations
- Good palette support
- Import/export palettes facilities
- Support for TWAIN and/or ISIS standards for scanners etc.
- Built-in image management

Usability requirements checklist

- Ease of use – if you are only an occasional user it may be easy to forget how to perform a routine operation in a complex package.
- Expected learning curve.
- Standardised interface to ease learning
- Good help features and available technical support.
- Third party books available
- Other possible imaging software requirements

Image manipulation is an area that really brings the 'art' into digital image creation, even for information-based resources. It can be important for the operator to have a keen sense of colour and proportion etc. and an affinity with the subject, as well as technical imaging knowledge and skills.

3.5 IMAGE CAPTURE EQUIPMENT: SCANNERS

Scanners are the most popular image capture device for digitising *existing image material*, e.g. slides, photographs, transparencies etc. This section aims to provide background information on scanners to aid appropriate choice of equipment for a digitisation project's needs. This is achieved by reviewing:

- Scanner types
- Scanner features/parameters
- Scanner interfaces

Introducing scanner types

Scanners come in several forms including:

- flatbed
- film
- drum

Each is discussed in detail later in this section.

Introducing scanner parameters

Factors to be considered when selecting an appropriate scanner include:

- Resolution
    Optical
    Interpolated
- Bit depth
- Scan area
- Scan times
- Colour accuracy
- Noise

Each factor will affect the quality of the final digital image. This is discussed in more detail below.

Introducing scanner interfaces

As well as the scanner itself it is also necessary to be aware of the various interfaces that are required to use a scanner with a computer. These include the:

- Hardware interface, which connects the scanner to the computer
- Driver/software interface, which operates the scanner

Scanners in detail

All scanners have the following components in common:

- Optical system (lenses etc.)
- Light sensor (detector array/Charge Couple Device – CCD)
- Driver software
- User interface

The specifications for these components and how they are arranged is what differentiates scanner types. The quality of scan obtainable is primarily dependent on the quality of the optical system and the light sensor, (detector array/CCD).

Scanner Types

- Flatbeds
    These are probably what most people first think of when they consider scanners. They are suitable for scanning printed papers, photographs and similar materials. With this type of scanner, the optical system moves the detector array/CCD past the image. Transparency adapters can be used to digitise films, X-rays and other transparent media.
    Typical resolutions range from 300 to 1000 dpi.
    Costs start at less than £100 and go to more than several thousand.

- Film/slide scanners
    Typically used for digitising photographic negatives and transparencies. These scanners normally move the film past a stationary scan head – this leads to a simpler and more compact system. There are film scanners capable of handling larger formats (4 inches x 5 inches etc), in addition to the more common 35mm slides. Advanced Photo System (APS), scanners are also on the market, some dedicated, others incorporating 35mm.

Typical resolutions are around 2700 dpi
Costs start at around £500 and rise to a few thousand.

- Drum scanners

  These are mainly the province of scanning bureaux and high quality professional work. They are high cost and require specialised skill to get the best from them. The drum can be loaded with several items at once and the driving software can separate the images from one another. Drum scanners usually need a dedicated workstation to handle the data rate and file sizes generated.

  Very high resolution – in excess of 4000dpi
  Costs start at around £15k

Scanner operating parameters

- Resolution
    - Optical
    - Interpolated
- Bit depth
- Scan area
- Scan times
- Colour accuracy
- Noiseglossary.html

1 Resolution

Resolution is measured in dots per inch (dpi). There are usually two figures given for resolution:
- Optical
- Interpolated

Optical resolution

This is the determining, and most important, factor, as it defines the maximum resolution possible at capture, without recourse to software 'approximations'.

For scanners that use Charge Coupled Devices (CCD) as the sensor, the optical resolution is limited by:

- The number of elements (pixels) in the detector array
- How the array is moved relative to the image (this does not apply to scanners using video CCDs).

Interpolated resolution

Use interpolation with care: the interpolated resolution is a figure that results from the scanner software 'estimating' the value(s) between pixels and presenting these intermediate values as a 'real' value. The quality of the results obtained is dependent on how the scanner software performs the interpolation and the type of image content.

Most scanner interpolation is performed within the scanner itself and the user can have little or no control. An alternative is to use image manipulation software to interpolate after primary capture.

Image software interpolation, though usually slower than scanner-interpolation, offers potentially greater quality and control, as the method used can be selected on a per image basis. The overhead of storing and transferring larger files, which contain estimated values, against performing these tasks in software later if deemed necessary, should be considered when weighing up using interpolation.

For high quality imaging it is recommended that scanners are selected for their optical resolution capacities and to capture as per optical resolution, rather than an interpolated resolution, which can be achieved at a later date, if necessary.

2 Bit depth

This parameter controls the ultimate colour (or greyscale) resolution, i.e. the ability to 'see' details in shadow or highlight areas of an image. At the 'consumer' end of the market the majority of scanners are 24bit although 30bit is becoming more common. The figure may also be given as an optical density value (OD); this is a logarithmic scale of brightness (see Table below).

A good quality photographic *print* will have a contrast range of around 100:1; therefore, the benefits of higher bit sampling scanners is minimal – although they are likely to decrease noise.

30bit and above scanners show an advantage in the digitisation of transparent materials e.g. negatives; transparencies, including *slides* and X-rays. Transparencies may have contrast ratios in the region of 300:1 and X-rays in excess of 500:1. Because the extra information comes from being able to 'see' further into the dark areas of the image it is 'shadow' details that improve the most.

The following table shows the relationship between photographic optical density and other values and greyscale bit-depth.

3 Scan area

Most flatbed scanners have a scanning area of about 8.5 inches by 12–14 inches. This covers the most common standard paper sizes. Transparency adapters may come with a mask that reduces the imaging area to that of the transparency. Flatbed scanners that handle larger paper sizes (e.g. A3) are also available.

Some flatbed scanners have the useful addition of dual optics, where the optical system can be switched to scan a half-width strip at twice the normal resolution.

Dedicated film scanners usually have a scan area that is the size of a 35mm slide/negative. Again there are scanners designed to handle the larger formats. Scanners for the new Advanced Photographic System (APS) are also on the market, sometimes combined with a 35mm scanner.

Optical density	%transmitted / reflected	contrast range	Approximate bit equivalent (greyscale)
0	100	0	-
1	10	10:1	3-4
2	1	100:1	7
3	0.1	1000:1	10

Table 2: Comparison of optical density, transmittance, contrast range and bit depth

4 Scan times

Not all scanners will take the same time to scan the same image at the same resolution. If throughput is important, check the scanner specification for times for *both* 'preview' and 'full scan' images. If possible, use a representative sample of the material you intend to digitise on an identical or similar system to the one you intend to use. If the scanner comes with an automatic sheet feeder for batch processing (see below), check the effect this has on scan times.

Most scanners are now single pass. However, earlier scanners, especially the budget ones, were often triple pass when colour scanning. This was because the CCD was a single pixel deep, so that the first pass would take place with a red filter (for example) over the CCD, green on the next pass and blue on the final pass. Thus three passes to build up a colour image will take three times longer than a greyscale scan.

5 Colour accuracy

For some users this parameter may be as important as resolution and bit depth.

A number of scanners come with colour management software (CMS). This software helps to *'close the loop'* between the analogue image being scanned, 'primary acquisition image' and delivery surrogates, so that the fidelity to the original image is maximised throughout.

The competency and complexity of the colour management software is usually reflected in the scanner price, although some of the software can be bought separately. Higher quality software also tends to come with better quality calibration targets for scanning. For further details on CMS see Section 3.7

Very high colour accuracy requirements may need colour densitometers for best results.

6 Noise

All electronic devices suffer from (electronic) noise to a greater or lesser extent. Noise is electronic interference that can cause inaccuracies in images. In scanners this noise has its greatest effect in low light level detection, i.e. when scanning the dark areas of images.

This is another reason why higher quality 30/36bit scanners can give better results – they tend to use higher quality (lower noise) components. Often going unnoticed in 'routine' scanning, noise is most likely to show itself when shadow areas of an image are lightened or have their contrast range increased. If the noise in a scanner is particularly bad it will mask shadow detail. Old light sources in a scanner can also aggravate the problem as well as affecting colour accuracy. All of the above factors will affect the quality of the final digital image.

It is also very important to calibrate the whole system from input (scanners etc.) to output (monitors, printers etc.).See Section 3.7.

Optional extra features for scanners

Two optional features are:

- Transparent media adapter (TMA)
- Automatic sheet feeder (ASF)

Transparent media adapter (TMA)

A TMA may well remove the need to buy a dedicated film scanner, if digitising 35mm slides/ negatives at a low resolution, say 600dpi.

Automatic sheet feeder (ASF)

The ASF is really only for those who need to batch process quantities of single sheets (bound/stapled documents will need to be separated into individual pages). If the pages to be digitised are double-sided, then an ASF that does duplexing will be necessary

Some film scanners can have automatic slide feeders for batch processing.

Scanner interfaces in detail

Scanner interfaces enable the device to be used with a computer. They include:

- Hardware interface, which connects the scanner to the computer
- Driver/software interface, which operates the scanner

Hardware interfaces

This is the way that the image capture device connects to the computer. Connection type affects both performance and support issues, examples include:

- SCSI
- ECP
- Serial
- USB
- FireWire

1 SCSI

Mainly due to the data rates involved in scanning, and its cross-platform compatibility, SCSI is usually the interface of choice.

2 ECP

The Enhanced Capabilities Port (ECP) lowers the cost of the scanner and increases portability between computers. It is especially useful for laptop users. If it is a parallel pass-through connection, this means that the printer can still be used with the scanner plugged in.

3 Serial

Some low data-rate scanners use serial connections but these are generally too slow for anything other than occasional use.

4 USB

Ideally suited for low-to mid-range scanners, the Universal Serial Bus (USB) is supported by some scanner manufacturers as a low cost, reasonably fast data rate, 'hot pluggable' (able to be plugged in without turning off the computer) connection.

5 FireWire

High end scanners may well feature a FireWire (P1394) interface, capable of data transfer speeds of up to 100Mbps.

Driver/Software interface

Introducing scanner driver software interfaces

Interface software, known as a device driver, is used to control the imaging hardware and retrieve the image data. The driver is specific to a particular device (or family of devices). Standard driver interfaces, e.g. TWAIN and ISIS, exist to reduce the problem of each application needing its own specific driver for each piece of hardware.

In addition to the expected features of setting resolution, scan area and colour/greyscale, most of these drivers do not just grab the image and pass it on to an application; they generally offer some form of image manipulation/processing and often quite a substantial amount.

Examples of the type of processing that may be performed by the driver are:

- contrast/brightness adjustment
- film type colour correction
- gamma correction
- colour cast removal
- positive/negative image selection
- Image rotation (portrait to landscape)
- descreening (removal of the matrix of dots in printed material)

Using these facilities while acquiring the image can save a lot of time in corrective manipulation later on, but care should be taken to ensure no significant information is lost.

The ability to save acquisition settings for different source material, e.g. A5 colour photographs or A4 line art, can also give further time savings and greater image consistency.

Types of driver software

- TWAIN
- ISIS

TWAIN

This is an interface between image acquisition hardware and image manipulation applications. It is extensible and platform independent.

The specification allows multiple sources to be installed at one time, the users choosing which source they wish to select from the application's menu. The user can then set scanning/acquisition options (these options may vary widely from device to device).

Normally it would be expected that the TWAIN source would be a hardware device (e.g. scanner, digital camera, frame grabber) but virtual devices, such as an image databases, are also allowed.

ISIS

This driver, though not as widespread as TWAIN, offers a number of advantages. ISIS is implemented as a series of modules connected as pipes. This architecture allows the image data to be sent to multiple destinations, while simultaneously performing other operations on the data, such as compression, format conversion, file writing etc. Data is handled in 8KB 'chunks' and this means that, among other things, big image files may be handled without requiring large amounts of RAM.

This way of handling the data may reduce 'bottlenecks' and, consequently, speed up scanning.

Whichever combination of acquisition device(s) and application(s) is chosen, take time to understand the settings available in the device driver(s).

3.6 IMAGE CAPTURE EQUIPMENT: DIGITAL CAMERAS

Introducing digital cameras

A digital camera's prime use is for capturing 'real time' events or objects in situ. However, digital cameras can also be used as per a 'rostrum camera', to capture existing 'image-objects', such as prints etc. This section discusses:

- Types of digital camera available
- Digital camera parameters/features
- Digital camera 'extras'
- Comparing digital and film cameras for resource creation purposes

Types of digital camera

There are a number of ways to group digital cameras, e.g. by cost, resolution, image capacity and so on. Herein, *type and arrangement of the detector* (light sensing device) are considered as this tends to dominate cost, performance and functionality.

Two main types of detector are currently used in digital cameras

- CCD (Charge Coupled Device)
- CMOS (Complementary Metal Oxide Semiconductor).

CCD (Charge Coupled Device)

CCD detectors are by far the most common and should represent the standard for image capture for information-based resources, because of the higher quality images they are capable of producing.

CMOS (Complementary Metal Oxide Semiconductor)

These are the cheaper type of detectors and their use is likely to increase although this will almost certainly be restricted to the budget end of the market, due in part to the 'noisier' images generated by current versions of the detector.

For the remainder of this section all references to detectors are to CCD devices, unless specifically stated otherwise.

Detector arrangement

Detector arrangement includes:

- The layout of the light detecting elements within the detector array
- The optical configuration of the array.

There are three main types of detector arrangement:

- Area array
- Scanning linear array
- Scanning area array

1 Area array cameras

The first and most common arrangement is the area array, Fig. 1. In this type of detector there is a fixed number of vertical and horizontal pixels. Higher resolution cameras use more expensive arrays containing more pixels. During image capture the whole array is exposed at once.

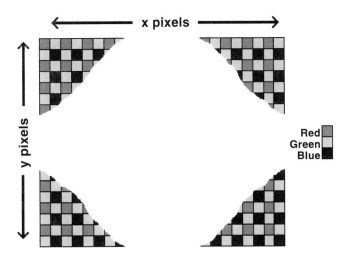

Figure 1: Area array detector arrangement

Area array camera features

- Costs: from budget to high end of the market
- Generally small, robust and portable
- Usually come with built-in storage for the image files
- High end area array cameras are often built around high quality 35mm camera bodies
- Suitable for moving subjects (light levels/exposure time permitting)
- Can be used with flash lighting
- Can have higher frame rates than cameras using other detector arrangements, up to 1 frame per second more.
- Easy to use, i.e. very similar to film cameras

3–chip area array cameras

A variation on the area array is the 3–chip camera. These use three individual area array detectors, each one receiving either red, green or blue light (the light having being separated into these components by some form of dispersion element).

3–chip cameras are high-end devices with image quality a major feature, but using three detectors and the necessary additional components inevitably increases cost and size.

2 Scanning linear array cameras

Digital cameras using this type of detector, Fig. 2, can be considered similar to flatbed scanners, with a lens replacing the flat glass plate. The array is moved across the imaging plane by a stepper motor. Most linear arrays use a tri-linear array (three rows of detectors), for simultaneous detection of red, green and blue (RGB). Resolution is limited by the number of cells along the array and, in the other direction, by stepper motor resolution.

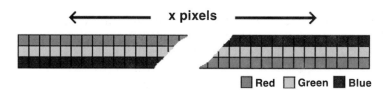

Figure 2: Linear array detector arrangement

Scanning linear array camera features

- Capture times are similar to flatbed scanners, often measured in minutes per image
- Long image acquisition times mean this type of camera is *not* usually suited to capturing moving objects and flash lighting is not feasible
- These are normally high-resolution devices (in terms of pixel count) which leads to large image files, meaning that the image is not usually stored in the camera but is sent directly to a computer
- Coupled with the need for mains power and larger size, these are *transportable* rather than portable devices
- Higher skill level required to achieve best results

3 Scanning area array

This technique is a hybrid of the previous two – an area array (Fig. 1) is moved in the horizontal and vertical planes to build up a potentially very high-resolution image.

Scanning area array camera features

- Very high resolutions possible, as the detector is no longer limited to the number of pixels that linear or area arrays can be manufactured with
- Comparatively limited portability, storage and speed
- Higher degree of skill level required achieve best results

Digital camera parameters/features

Factors to be considered when selecting an appropriate digital camera include:

- Resolution
- Memory and compression
- Noise
- Dynamic range
- Colour accuracy
- Image transfer/Interfaces
- Practicality/usability

1 Digital cameras and resolution

Resolution applies, in the main, to *area array* cameras; it is much less common in scanning array specifications, as it is not so fixed with the latter.

With digital cameras, resolution is most often given in terms of 'Interpolated resolution', not 'optical resolution' (see Section 3.5 for a full explanation of these terms). This means that comparison of quoted resolution figures can be misleading, as the exact array-layout, ratios, interpolation and compression algorithms used can vary from camera model to camera model.

For example, one of the vogue terms for comparing digital cameras is 'megapixel' resolution; essentially this means that the image is made up of (at least) 1 million pixels. The implication here is that the more pixels, the higher the resolution, i.e. more detail captured, and the higher the resulting image quality, but this is *not* necessarily so, if varying interpolation methods are being employed.

Wherever possible, refer to optical resolutions for more objective comparison of area-array digital cameras.

2 Digital cameras: memory and compression

Digital image files are' memory hogs'. A true 'megapixel' 24bit uncompressed colour image would take up 3MB of storage. The *flash* memory used in digital cameras is relatively expensive (currently about £100 for 12MB, enough to hold four of the above images). For this reason most 'consumer' digital cameras store their images in a *compressed* form in the cameras' memory.

This compression is nearly always of the JPEG type, i.e. lossy (see section 3.2 for an explanation of compression). The exact algorithm used internally will vary from camera to camera. These algorithms are designed to minimise visual loss, that is they discard information which is less noticeable to the human visual system. Exactly how noticeable the compression is will vary from camera to camera and also depends on image content. Most cameras also offer two or more levels of compression, trading quality for number of images.

3 Digital cameras and noise

All electronic equipment can suffer from 'noise' – unwanted input. Noise is used here in the sense of pixels in the digital image containing incorrect values. Noise of this type shows up particularly at low lighting levels. At low lighting levels, ensure flash/auxiliary lighting is used.

Apart from detracting from image quality, noise can cause additional problems when the camera software compresses the image because it is incorporating something which shouldn't really be there.

If subjects are often taken under low light levels, try a range of cameras suited to these conditions. The specification to pay attention to here is the sensitivity (normally given in lux) or the ISO film speed equivalent. Also, larger aperture lenses let more light through to the detector.

Currently CMOS sensors have poorer noise performance than standard CCD devices.

4 Dynamic range

This is a measure of the range of tones between the highlights and shadows in an image. In conventional photography this is measured in stops (a stop equals a factor of 2 in brightness, e.g. 5 stops = 32 times brightness difference, 10 stops = 1024 times). For digital cameras it is normally represented by the bit depth, usually 24bits.

Whether the ability to handle a wide dynamic range is important or not will depend very much on individual circumstances. Currently most consumer digital cameras can capture the equivalent of 7 or 8 stops of contrast. Film generally has a wider range, dependent on film type, processing etc.

5 Colour accuracy

Colour accuracy can be simple or complicated to achieve for all cameras, depending in part on how much the lighting is under control.

Most films are well characterised in their response to different wavelengths; couple this with readily available colour temperature meters and correction filters and there is a fair degree of control available. However, results are not seen until the film comes back from processing. Very similar results would be expected from different cameras using the same film/lighting/processing combinations.

For digital cameras there is not yet the same degree of colour specification information. Most digital cameras attempt to correct for different light sources but how effective this is will depend on a number of factors including:

- The filters used in the array
- The internal image processing
- The nature of the lighting

If colour accuracy is essential to the work being carried out, check for the availability of ICC profiles or consider making your own. Also check to see if the camera offers a manual white balance option. (See Section 3.7).

Do not yet expect anything like the same degree of colour conformity with digital cameras as is available with film.

6 Image transfer

Having used a camera to capture images, the images will normally need to be transferred to a computer for viewing, archiving, manipulating, etc. Image data is normally transferred in compressed form and expanded on receipt. This can be achieved either by:

- Direct image transfer
- Using memory/storage media

Direct image transfer
This requires a hardware interface port, such as:

- Serial
- Parallel
- SCSI
- USB (Universal Serial Bus)

Serial
This is probably the most common interface, as it is found on almost every computer and there are few compatibility problems. It has one major drawback and that is its relatively slow speed. The usual maximum data rate is 115k bits per second. If you are transferring lots of large image files via a serial link it is worth checking the batch transfer capabilities of the interface software, and supporting application, if it is by a TWAIN driver.

Parallel

This is not as common as serial, but has potentially higher speed, 100k bytes per second. Printer pass-through may be available to allow the simultaneous attachment/use of printer and camera.

SCSI

This is the 'standard' interface for scanning linear/area array cameras because of the amount of data that can be transferred, but is also available on some high-end area array cameras. Data rates vary from 5MB per second for SCSI1 up to 20MB for SCSI2.

USB (Universal Serial Bus)

This is a recent interface standard that is slowly becoming more widely supported. It has a number of distinct advantages: high-speed 12Mbps (Megabits per second); low cost; ubiquitous, on most recent computers; hot-pluggable (i.e. devices can be plugged and unplugged without turning the computer off); up to 127 devices per USB port; power can be taken from powered hubs.

Some cameras are equipped with more than one interface standard, often one for maximum compatibility, e.g. serial, and another for higher speed, e.g. USB.

Image transfer via memory/storage media
These include:

• Memory cards
• Discs

Memory cards

Memory cards come in a range of capacities, currently 2–48MB, and can be useful for transferring one set of images whilst the camera, with another memory card, is being used to take more pictures. They come in a few different types, including:

• PCCard
• Compact Flash
• SmartMedia

Some adapters are available including those for:

• Reading Compact Flash and SmartMedia cards via PCCard slot on a laptop
• Reading via 3.5 inch disc drives
• External direct connection to a computer (CompactFlash)

Discs

A few years ago a couple of the early digital cameras, Canon Ion, Sony Mavica, used 3.5" floppy discs to store images. This was discontinued in later cameras until Sony recently released a new Mavica using 3.5" floppy discs. The main advantages are:

- Low cost
- Readily available storage
- Ease of transfer

The disadvantages include:

- Power consumption, for disc drive motor
- Speed (slow to save each image)
- Low capacity, therefore low resolution/quality images.

It has been mooted that some of the high capacity floppy 'replacements', e.g. ZIP, LS120, would make suitable future drives for this purpose, although power consumption would still be a problem.

It is worth ensuring that the camera you intend using has some way of getting the images onto all the computers it is likely to be used with. Also check multiple-use license conditions.

7 Digital camera 'usability' considerations

In addition to the more technical matters discussed above, there are the following specifications which are more 'usability' oriented. These include:

- Batteries
- Viewfinders
- Lens capabilities
- Flash
- User/camera controls

Batteries

All *portable* digital cameras use batteries as their primary power source, but most can use battery eliminators when a mains supply is available. The purchase of batteries can be a significant running cost for some cameras, especially those that use non-standard lithium cells. Some cameras can use rechargeable NiCad cells in addition to normal zinc-carbon or manganese alkaline cells.

There are a number of factors affecting battery life, such as:

- Motor functions (zooming, focusing)
- Flash
- LCD screens
- Image transfers

Heavy use of these facilities can drastically reduce battery life (to less than an hour in some instances). Most cameras include automatic power down after a period of inactivity (i.e. they turn themselves off or go on standby). It is always a good policy to have spares available.

Viewfinders

There are essentially three types of viewfinder on digital cameras:

- Standard real image optical finder
- TTL/SLR (Through the lens/single lens reflex)
- LCD (Liquid Crystal Display)

Standard real image optical finder
This is the most common finder on budget cameras (both film and digital). Its advantages are:

- Low cost
- No power consumption (as non electronic), unless coupled to a zoom lens
- Works well under a range of lighting conditions
- Image is always available

Disadvantages are:

- The finder does not show exactly what the lens sees
- The offset from the lens leads to easy misalignment, especially at close range
- Depth of field (the degree of front to back focus) can't be previewed.

TTL/SLR (through the lens/single lens reflex)
These comprise a more complex optical system. The main advantages are:

- The finder (as the name implies) shows exactly what the lens sees
- Low power consumption (as non electronic)

Disadvantages include:

- Cost
- Weightier than other systems
- Image disappears during exposure (the exception to this are cameras using pellicle lenses – a beam splitter system)

LCD viewfinders
These are often used in conjunction with a standard optical finder, less often with the TTL/SLR viewfinders, for which it is often a substitute.
   Advantages to LCD viewfinders include:

- Shows what the detector is seeing (cf. TTL)
- Works well under low light levels
- Often movable, enabling viewing/composition when the camera is in awkward position
- Permits previewing/reviewing and possibly deletion of images

Disadvantages:

- Power consumption (especially important if it is the only viewfinder fitted or cannot be turned off)
- Does not usually work well under bright light conditions
- Can be poor resolution/low image quality

Lens capabilities

'Special' function lenses

A number of cameras are fitted with lenses that go beyond the simple fixed focus, fixed focal length lenses of the budget cameras. The most common of these added features are:

- Zoom lenses
- Macro lenses
- Interchangeable lenses

Zoom lenses

Optical zoom is probably the most popular lens feature on consumer cameras. Normally the zoom range is restricted to around 3:1. On the cheaper cameras, there is a trade-off in maximum aperture at longer focal lengths, e.g. zooming in means that the camera's low light level performance may suffer.

Some cameras use a digital zoom (or a combination of the two). Digital zooming involves further interpolation and usually leads to a degradation in image quality.

Macro lenses

These allow the camera to get in closer to the subject: a non-macro lens' closest focus will normally be around 50–70cm, a macro lens will often come in to 25cm or less.

Interchangeable lenses

These are normally only found on the high-end cameras. They enable the lens to be changed according to the needs of the subject. Not only is the camera more expensive, but there is also the extra cost of the additional lenses to consider. The advantages of interchangeable lenses are:

- Higher quality is usually obtained from a lens designed for a specific purpose than from one which is a 'jack-of-all-trades'
- Lenses for specific functions can be fitted, e.g. extreme macro or wide-angle lenses, as required.

Flash

This is *common on area array* cameras, but *not* fitted on scanning cameras.

Camera control

This can vary greatly, from no control, e.g. fixed/auto focus, auto exposure, auto flash, to fairly comprehensive control, e.g. exposure, aperture, film speed equivalent, focus etc. Some cameras will carry both as options. The range of circumstances under which the pictures will be taken will be a major factor in determining how much control is needed.

A number of cameras allow computer control. This can be useful for:

- Taking images remotely
- Imaging at set intervals
- Transferring image data immediately after exposure

The amount of control obtainable will vary from camera to camera. Scanning array cameras are usually operable only under computer control.

Digital camera 'extras'

These include:

- Picture annotation
- TV out

Picture annotation

Some cameras allow sound to be recorded, normally at the expense of image capacity. These 'memos' can be used as on-the-spot records of subject, exposure details and so on.

TV out

A number of digital cameras are fitted with a 'TV out' socket allowing the camera to be connected to a normal domestic television set (check standards! PAL/NTSC etc.). This can be useful for image review without transfer to a computer. Note that the quality of television display will compromise high resolution/quality images.

Whichever type and specification of camera you use, the whole system – scanners, monitors, printers etc. – should also be calibrated. (For more information about calibration see Section 3.7.)

Comparing digital and film cameras for resource creation purposes

The sections above made some comparisons between the capabilities of digital cameras and conventional film cameras. This final section provides some more direct comparisons of the proficiencies of digital and film cameras for image creation for inclusion in high quality digital information resources for the visual arts. For in situ/real time imaging needs, there are currently two options:

- Directly capture with a digital camera
- Capture with a conventional camera and digitise the results with a scanner.

1 Directly capturing with a digital camera

On the proviso that the camera selected will provide the quality of images necessary for the purposes required (likely to be a 'scanning' type camera), the advantages of this method are:

- A 'one-stop' digitisation solution
- Allows for speedy review of results
- Immediate ability to manipulate the captured image, either via integral display or download/ view on computer

Disadvantages are:

- Likely higher initial cost of suitable equipment
- Greater operator skill required
- Relatively new and not so 'established' media
- Limited image storage (memory, if expandable, is fairly costly)

- No inherent archivable hard copy
- Normally low repeat frame rate, due to time required for compression.

2. Capturing with a conventional camera, then digitising the results with a scanner

Advantages:

- Additional analogue source for 'archiving'/'delivery' requirements is obtained.
- Less expensive for same or higher quality image results.
- Well understood and widely supported medium.
- Essentially unlimited image capacity – easy to carry extra film
- Immediate archivable format
- Different film types available for varying circumstances; daylight, artificial light, fast, slow etc.

Disadvantages

- Multi step process
- Delay in seeing results (Polaroid excepted)
- Delay in ability to manipulate for varying purposes
- Long-term 'running' costs can be high

Range of costs

Initial costs for film cameras are much lower than even the cheapest digital cameras (single-use film cameras are available for under £10; currently the cheapest digital camera is about £100). Of course initial costs are only a part of the equation – there are a wide range of additional costs, some essential, some optional – that need to be taken into consideration. These include:

For film cameras:

- Film; processing
- Accessories – necessary/optional, e.g. lenses, cases, filters etc.
- Batteries/power supply
- Maintenance
- Film storage/archiving
- Digitisation costs

For digital cameras:

- Batteries/power supply
- Memory
- Accessories – optional/needed, e.g. lenses, cases, filters etc.
- Transfer to archival medium

How these comparisons/costs break down will vary widely according to circumstances, i.e. the weighting applied to these factors is dependent upon the project's needs, and some things will be difficult to assess/cost, e.g. the importance of immediacy and final image quality. As a guide, work out costs per image, taking the above points into account, multiply this by projected annual image rate and add initial equipment expense.

3.7 IMAGE DIGITISATION PROCESS: WORK FLOW, PROCEDURES AND GOOD PRACTICES

Introducing the production process

Choosing whether to undertake digital image creation 'internally', which may require recruiting specialist staff and equipment, or to 'out-source' it, will usually be influenced by the volume of images to be created, the nature of the original objects to be digitised and the staff skills and technology already 'on-tap'.

Whichever route is taken, it is important to be aware of *good practices and procedures* in the actual *production process* of creating digital images.

The image digitisation process goes from identifying and assessing the original analogue sources, to producing a digital 'primary capture' image with accompanying metadata. The creation of surrogate 'archival/master' and 'delivery' images can be extended from this.

Quality Assurance mechanisms should be in place throughout the digitisation process to ensure minimum error and maximum consistency in the digital images created.

The total image digitisation process, or *work flow* can be separated into the following three phases, each subject to QA:

- Pre-digitisation feasibility study
- Digitisation
- Post-digitisation processes

1 Pre-digitisation feasibility study
This should:

- Assess the analogue originals for their suitability to be digitised
- Identify any special requirements of the analogue items, e.g. handling procedures
- Identify the most appropriate method of capture
- Establish benchmarks and procedures for image capture

2 Digitisation
This is the actual primary image capture procedure, including the application of initial metadata and storage of files. It also includes the preparation and handling of analogue originals prior to capture and on their return to their original source.

3 Post-digitisation processes
These include

- Backing-up and archiving 'primary image capture' files
- Creating 'archival/master digital image' surrogates and accompanying metadata, if not as per primary image capture file
- Adding metadata (can be achieved simultaneous to digitisation)
- Creating 'delivery' surrogates and accompanying metadata as necessary
- Writing 'surrogates' to storage and portable media
- Integrating 'delivery' images to user applications
- Archiving

Procedure guidelines for digitisation

These guidelines are adapted from a report on the experiences of both HEDS (Higher Education Digitisation Service: http://heds.herts.ac.uk/) and TASI in advising and guiding the JISC Image Digitisation Initiative (JIDI) project. The JIDI project relates to *large volume* digitisation of *existing* analogue resources, using *scanners* as the image capture device. The original report has been adapted herein for more generic application. The principles discussed can be transferred to other types of digital creation scenarios.

For the unedited JIDI workflow report see: http://www.tasi.ac.uk/building/workflow1.html
For the full JIDI Feasibility Study report see: http://heds.herts.ac.uk/Guidance/JIDI_fs.html
The guidelines below relate to the *digitisation* phase of the creation process, after a feasibility study and prior to any major post-digitisation processes, which the rest of the guide advises on. (The procedures are based upon and applicable to digitisation feasibility studies.)

Digitisation production procedures

Preparation

Good preparation of analogue originals and technical systems is essential to help avoid common errors or quality defects encountered in large scale digitisation projects. Preparation falls into two categories:

- Preparation of analogue materials – by the supplier/owner of originals before the materials are transferred to the digitisation site and their handling at the digitisation point
- Preparation of technical systems – at digitisation point, to all operating hardware and for identification/storage of digital image files

Preparation of analogue materials

Before the original items are transported to the site of digitisation (whether internal to the organisation or out-sourced) it is important that every individual item is in the best condition possible, clearly labelled and suitably packaged. This will speed operations at the digitisation point and enable the digitisation operator to differentiate between the originals. This is essential to name the files created accurately.

In addition, an *inventory* of materials for digitisation should be maintained, to be *reflected across the whole production process*. The inventory should be created by those supplying/ responsible for the analogue items. (Metadata records, if established, may be used as the basis of an inventory.)

The inventory should include:

- Date of 'dispatch'
- Name and address of the 'supplier' and contact details of the person responsible for the items
- Number of physical items delivered for digitisation
- Unique identifiers for each item
- Physical description of each item, e.g. size, media, number of pages/parts if relevant, whether in mount or other protective material and format

The inventory can be used to:
- Log materials into the digitisation process
- Check-off, annotate, and 'sign off' items as they pass through the process
- Log materials back to their source

A spreadsheet or simple database is useful for creating inventories, but it is also useful for the items to be accompanied by a *paper inventory* through all stages. This will aid checking-in, annotating, and 'signing off' items as they pass through the process.

The inventory can also be used as the basis for file creation and recording mechanisms for the management of originals through the digitisation process.

The inventory should be reflected back to the originating body at the point of digitisation, to ensure that all items have been safely received. There should likewise be a further inventory check at the point of return of materials to the originator.

An inventory is thus a useful management tool. It can provide a full record of all production processes undertaken on analogue items and their digital versions. It is recommended that however far or near (even in the same building) items are moved for digitisation, they should be fully inventoried to this level to ensure against loss or mistaken identification.

Packaging of originals
The 'supplier' of the original materials should be responsible for the packaging of the items for movement. This should be done with the distance and type of transport to be used in mind.

The fragility of materials and any special handling requirements should be clearly indicated, to prohibit damage, either in storage or in production.

Summary of preparation of analogue materials
All of the above factors help to ensure that no items are misplaced or damaged either in transit or during digitisation. It also ensures against errors in naming files created. Further, it makes quality assurance at all levels more efficient by providing easily comparable input records against the end product.

The recording mechanism (inventory) for the throughput of originals will need to be designed, possibly at the *media/format level*. The inventory can then enable *automatic filename creation* at the point of scanning, by picking filenames from a *pre-created list of materials to be processed*. This reduces scanner operator interpretation and reduces file naming errors.

The directory file structures for digital images should be created on the capture system *before* any scanning takes place to enable items to be placed easily into the correct data structures and again to reduce operator interpretation.

Every possible mechanism should be set up to ensure that the scan operators can concentrate their core skills on handling materials, scanning and producing acceptable images, and not on constructing filenames or data structures, which should be ready in place.

Preparation local to digitisation
Preparation of scanner capture systems and software settings
Every digitisation service will use different equipment in slightly different configurations, but there are some common themes and methods that can ensure the best set up.

Memory

On production equipment it is important to reduce the number of extraneous programs or memory resident applications that are running and to include only those that are going to assist in the digitisation process.

Scanning/manipulation software location

It is recommended that software resources required for scanning be locally available on the hard disk of the production machine, even if the machine is networked. (It may even be beneficial to disconnect the machine from a network during production.)

Environmental conditions

Light conditions can have a substantial effect on the ability of the operator to assess tones and colours accurately both in the originals and on screen. *Natural light* is preferable to artificial light, but should be controllable to allow the operator to modify conditions to suit the prevailing light conditions. Reflections and high light conditions should be avoided as they affect the fidelity of on-screen images.

Monitor considerations

The computer monitor configuration is important in gaining the most accurate results from the scanned images. The following are recommendations:

- Consider configuring the desktop to *grey* as this tone will not distract the eye
- Ensure that the display profile is set for 24 or 32bit (TrueColor) colours and the refresh rate is optimised for the display driver to reduce screen flicker to a minimum
- Aim for the highest possible desktop area resolution, greater than or equal to 1024x768 pixels, whilst not reducing the 24bit colour display capacity
- Check the profile of the monitor and use this profile to ensure the monitor is set to the optimum settings recommended by the manufacturer
- Using the monitor's own configuration menu, ensure that the colour temperature is suitable (6500 K recommended) and not over-bright
- Ensure that the screen area fills the monitor view area and is not skewed or trapezoid. This can be adjusted using the monitor's own configuration menus
- Use imaging or scan software that allows for monitor set-up to adjust the monitor to a reliable colour target (e.g. Kodak colour swatches). Ensure that the software is set to the manufacturers model and this should automatically set the monitors gamma value
- The imaging/scanning software white point should be the same as the screen's colour temperature.
- The phosphors settings should be set at the screen manufacturers' recommended setting
- The gamma setting can be modified in conjunction with colour management support against a reliable colour or greyscale target, but a value of 1.5 is normal for PC monitors

Colour management

Image digitisation should aim for accurate, repeatable, colour from the input phase through the display and to output. This is where Colour Management Software (CMS) is brought into play as the best means currently available for enabling colour matching.

Colour perception is complicated by environmental conditions, and by psychological and physical factors in the operator. CMS assists in reducing these factors to ensure more quantifiably accurate outputs by relating output to a standard colour definition.

There are a number of CMS packages and systems available. With this variation in CMS operating environments it is not possible to give a definitive 'how to' guide for using CMS, but there are some common features that should be utilised:

Colour and greyscale targets are provided by Kodak and enable the scanner and monitor to be configured to reproduce accurately the colours and tones on the target cards or slides. As the outputs are measurable against the targets, then scanner profiles can be created and saved to be used in production set-up.

Output profiles can be used and modified to ensure that the output conforms to the International Color Consortium (ICC) colour standard whilst replicating the colour of the original as accurately as possible.

Colour and greyscale targets can be used to 'record' the correct colour or tone of an original before it goes into the scanner. This provides a reference point when the original is no longer available in the scanner for direct viewing. The record can be compared to the displayed image to ensure the tone and colour representation in the recorded section is accurate.

Handling and optimising originals at scanner point
The handling of the originals has to be considered quite carefully and the digitisation *environment* must be the first step in ensuring safe handling. The recommendations for handling at the digitisation point are:

- Digitisation area must be clean and as dust free as practical
- Capture devices and PCs should be maintained to a very clean standard on a daily basis.
- Digitisation production areas must be food, drink and smoking free
- Protective gloves should ideally be worn at all times when handling originals. This helps ensure that no grease marks get on the original to mar the digital image or degrade the original
- There must be ample layout table space around the capture device. This space should equal the size of the largest storage box for the originals plus space on a separate surface for the original about to be digitised
- The capture device and PC should be arranged to ensure maximum ease of access so as to reduce handling accidents when placing originals in the equipment
- Operators must endeavour not to touch any of the actual original material surfaces and only handle the frame or mounting of the material

Slides and other transparencies can get quite dusty and hairs can attach. These can be removed with careful application of a clean air device such as a puff brush.

Loading the scanner with original materials
It is preferable to use multi-frame holders for 35mm slides and negatives as this enables quicker transference of originals into the scan area and reloading of the holders whilst the scan is taking place.

It is recommended that two transparency holders for each size and media be used to enable loading of one whilst the other is in use, optimising production times.

Images from originals to be scanned on flatbed devices are optimised by being weighted flat onto the scan bed. If this is an acceptable method for handling such materials, then backing paper or glass can be used to weight the original flat.

When doing flatbed scans of very large format originals, more than one person may be required to ensure the positioning and care of the original is maintained. A further person can operate the scanner as needed.

Technical issues for scanning

'Pre-scanning' techniques

Prior to capturing a digital image a 'pre-scan' is made to adjust and set the capture parameters in the scanner/imaging software. The following settings need to be established (for each scan, unless a scanning setting has been established for multiple items):

- 'White-point' (highlights)
- Brightness
- Shadows
- Cropping

1 White point (highlight)

These are the areas of the image which may be used to maintain a full range of tone values for the image. The 'white point' or highlight is taken from *the whitest area in the image with the most detail.* The white point function on the scanner can be set on this point in the image and the tone values for the image will be adjusted.

It is important to choose a good white point, preferably towards the centre of the image. Do not use specular/reflective or overexposed areas as highlight points.

If the scanner provides a histogram or densitometer function then add about 5–10% to the white point value to give a little headroom for other highlight areas in the image and to ensure their details are not lost in the output image.

2 Brightness

The overall 'weight' of the image is controlled by the brightness setting. Most scanners allow for adjustment of brightness or gamma that can lighten or darken the image. This function can help ensure that the colour saturation or tones of the image are closest to the target tones on the original. However, after adjustment it is essential to check the highlight and shadow settings as they may have been affected by any changes made.

3 Shadows

These are defined as areas of the image that are dark and contain the most detail. It is essential to maintain the maximum detail in dark areas without them becoming too black or looking greyer than they actually are in the original. On an RGB readout, values of around 7–10 would be considered usual.

This function is not quite as important as the white point value in the scanning device, but devices without this support will be more limited in adjustment capacity.

4 Cropping

The images on the preview scan can be optimised through cropping to ensure that only the original item is scanned and not the scanner bed, original mounting/frame or other extraneous matter.

It is essential that the cropping does not remove any information content from the original. For art images, a trained eye with subject knowledge will be able to make decisions about inclusion of frames and how to crop non-regular forms without jeopardising content.

Scanning

At this point all the adjustments that are deemed fit to best represent the original have been made and the original is ready to be scanned. The operator will get a fuller image to assess and ensure that the tonal range and the colours are representative of the origi

Scanning (QA): Quality Assurance

It is recommended that the first scan of a new item and media type is done at a quite low resolution and the results assessed for colour and tone fidelity against the original. This will provide useful guidance for further scanning from the collection and save time if any adjustment is required.

The operator should assess the image against the original or the colour target to assess accuracy of representation.

The operator should also look at the image's histogram to assess whether the highlight values have been 'stretched' or 'clipped', as this can affect the tonal range of the image and the level of information recorded.

When the operator is satisfied then the image can be saved to disk. If not satisfied then a re-scan is required.

A factor for 'bracketing'/'rescanning' should be accounted for in the budgeting of the digitisation process. This does not imply failure on the operator's part, but a realistic assessment of digitisation output.

Saving to disk and recording information

The output file should be created by saving the image to disk. The format for 'primary capture image' recommended is RGB in Uncompressed TIFF with the thumbnail option activated.

A recommended directory structure for primary capture images is:

> Resource/Project Name
>> —> Unique identifier of original
>>> —> Version numbered files.

This would work quite well for organising the output of an imaging project as a whole. However, bear in mind that each filename should be unique to each digital image. No filenames should be repeated otherwise confusion about the identity of digital images will result.

Adding technical image metadata

Technical image metadata are the data which describe the digital image itself, e.g. format, resolution, file-size etc. They can also include 'capture' details, such as creation date, creator (scanner operator).

Technical image metadata can be noted throughout the scanning process, as the relevant information becomes available, e.g. scan pixel dimension can be taken at the scan point from the software display, and the complete record added at the point where the 'primary capture image' is written to disk.

Image metadata should be entered onto a separate machine/storage space to enable the scan station to remain free for continuous production.

Every resource creation project will record varying levels of image metadata and hence may require different methodologies to keep the scan production process free of interruption. (For information on metadata relating to the intellectual content of the image, see Section 4.)

Writing to media (production-data storage and data delivery)

This section deals with two aspects of writing data to media:

- Storage of captured images in the production environment
- Transfer of digital images created

1 Storage of captured images in the production environment

Hard disk space on production machines is precious. It may therefore be required to write production data to another storage device or portable storage medium on a regular basis to free production resources.

Transferring such data volumes across a network may be detrimental to the network performance. In an ideal situation, this could be written in overnight processes. However, this may not be possible; thus a local or portable storage medium is recommended to move the data quickly and free up production resources.

2 Transfer of digital images created

The sending of data of large volume and file size would be untenable for FTP or other networked solutions. The most efficient method is to write to a hard medium that is agreed by the parties involved.

CD-ROM is fairly standard, but each disk can take up to 15 minutes to write, the failure rate for the media is quite high and large data volumes would create a very large number of CD-ROMs. This adds to the costs and also the chances of data being missed in the delivery of the end product.

Recommended transfer media is thus one which holds more data than a CD-ROM such as JAZ drive formats.

(See Section 7.1, storage and media issues, for a wider discussion of storage issues.)

Return of originals

Often forgotten about in arranging workflow is the handling of originals when they are returned to their sites of origin. Originals need to be checked against inventories both when leaving the digitisation point and on return to their source, to ensure that all are present and free of damage.

On their return to 'suppliers', originals, as well as being checked, will also need to be reintegrated into their storage systems. Time should be accounted for this in any planning.

QA procedures on completed datasets

Depending on the digitisation scenario regarding how closely the original source providers and digitisation point are connected, this may need to be carried out at either the digitisation point and/or the original source point.

Newly created digital image files should be subjected to QA procedures to assess the *fidelity* of the images against the originals, to discover any digitisation anomalies and to ensure filenames and any metadata added are correct for the corresponding image.

There is a cost balance to be made in whether every capture file is to be opened and viewed in detail or even superficially. This is usually considered prohibitively expensive, but for collections which have many distinct items it could be considered appropriate.

A 15% random sample on all images created is recommended as a suitable proportion to pick up systemic defects or problems with operator technique. This would enable a focused check on certain file areas, should a problem become apparent.

The equipment and software for quality assurance should be able to load, view and provide information on the image files quickly.

QA checks

For QA checks on individual newly created digital images, *access to the originals is appropriate*. QA should include looking for the following:

* Does the output file named correspond to the correct original object?
* Does the image include the requisite information in the original image? For example, has too much or too little cropping occurred?
* Does the digital image represent the tonal range and colours of the original accurately?
* Does the digital image conform to the agreed file standards in the specification?
* Does the information recorded about the image accurately represent the technical image information?
* Does the number of digital files delivered match the the number of analogue originals provided.

A workflow diagram, adapted from the JIDI reports, and depicting the primary image capture sequence is available in Appendix 2.

For the complete *workflow diagrams* specific to the JIDI Project, see either of the following documents:

> http://www.tasi.ac.uk/building/workflow1.html
> http://heds.herts.ac.uk/Guidance/JIDI_fs.html

The capture/digitisation phase of the digital image creation process will result in the 'primary capture image', and its accompanying metadata being achieved. This is the key content-creation exercise for digital image creation for visual arts resources.

However, it is only a part of the overall resource creation project, coming after planning and rights management has been completed and alongside or prior to the establishment of metadata and delivery and archive systems. The remainder of this guide considers the other areas of resource creation.

The procedures outlined above, coupled with the information in the preceding sections, should act as a guide to help ensure that high quality digital images suitable for a project's needs can be planned for and achieved, with requisite insights into the issues involved. Idiosyncrasies related to some projects may, however, benefit from individual consultancy on their digital image requirements. (See Appendix 1 for a list of useful organisations.)

Section 4: Standards for Data Documentation

SECTION 4.1 INTRODUCING STANDARDS FOR DATA DOCUMENTATION

The way in which electronic resources are described or documented is potentially fraught with conceptual and theoretical problems. This section therefore aims to clarify the key issues and give guidance about how to select and implement a suitable data documentation method for visual arts material.

Why is good documentation essential

Firstly, in networked environments the pieces of information you use to describe your resource is all that is available to interested researchers to locate it. If this information is inaccurate, misleading or idiosyncratically devised, potential barriers are erected to its effective use.

Secondly, much of the work you are likely to be doing when creating a digital resource will be in the realm of documentation and you are likely to invest a lot of time and energy in this process.

Example: A slide collection of Victorian silver is being digitised. Apart from creating digital images, you will need to devise a suitable way to provide textual information about each image. Ideally you would want to get this information correct from the outset. Selecting a suitable standard on which to base your documentation is a way of ensuring this.

You may be in a situation where you are working solely from what is inscribed on the slide mount itself. Alternatively, as an expert or scholar working on the subject of the resource you may wish to devise your own way of cataloguing the slides. However, because we are working in an environment which is becoming increasingly networked, the use of standards is becoming more practical and more essential.

Standards allow information to be exchanged between different electronic databases or catalogues and it is the use of common resource documentation standards that enhance this process.

What are the confusing issues

- Deciding which entity the data actually describe
- Providing electronic information about electronic information

1 Deciding which entity the data actually describe

This is a case of deciding between descriptors of varying levels and for varying needs. Continuing with the above example: in order for someone to retrieve an image from an electronic catalogue created from slides illustrating Victorian silver, we would expect the researcher to want to search on information about the object itself, including:

- The maker of a piece
- The hallmark which it holds
- The stylistic influences represented

We are less likely to expect them to want to find out 'collection data', for example:

- Who scanned the slide
- The file-size of the digital image
- The negative number of the photograph from which the slide originated

However, in order to create a consistent catalogue of electronic text and digital images, the latter kind of collection management information is absolutely crucial to the production process and so should be recorded (though not necessarily for users to search on).

We may also be faced with a situation where it is important to differentiate between, and provide information about, many different 'entities' which all derive from the same original source.

For example, for just one of the items in the electronic resource referred to above (a teapot, say) there could be all of the following entities:

i) The teapot itself – (on display currently at the V&A)

ii) An engraving of the teapot (in the V&A print room)

iii) A photograph of the engraving of the teapot (filed separately)

iv) A slide of the photograph of the engraving of the teapot (filed separately)

v) A digitised version of the slide of the photograph of the engraving of the teapot (the new digital record)

Potentially, all of these could be described separately at the time of creating the documentation. However, pragmatic decisions would need to be made at the time of digitisation about what is important enough to record, i.e. what is needed to manage the digital collection effectively and what the user may wish to retrieve on.

For example, problems can arise when a photograph of a work of art, as well as the object itself, is of scholarly interest or importance. In this case for the sake of simplicity a decision would need to be made about what information is the most important.

Some data documentation standards are more geared up than others to describe such complex multi-level resources. But however flexible they are, it is important to keep in mind at all times which entity, whether digital or non-digital, the data documentation is actually describing. It is also crucial to keep these issues clear for the users who are attempting to access the data. Decisions about what information you want users to access will have to be made.

This is a key issue to resolve, especially when employing a standard like the *Dublin Core* which is essentially geared up to one level of descriptive information about all the entities which you might want to discover on the Internet. The use and importance of the Dublin Core is described at greater length in Section 4.3.

2 Providing electronic information about electronic information

Confusion can arise when the documentation you are creating is about something which is already in electronic form. For example, you may be using a standard like MARC or the Dublin Core to provide information in your webpages about the electronic catalogue that you have created on Victorian silverware and made searchable via the Internet. Therefore essentially what you are providing is digital data about digital data (rather than digital data about actual works of art, or things that exist in analogue form like photographs).

The term that has been coined for this kind of documentation is Metadata.

SECTION 4.2 DOMAIN SPECIFIC DATA DOCUMENTATION STANDARDS

How to select a standard

It is difficult to offer very specific guidance and recommend one of the many standards available; it is usually more viable to offer advice on a case by case basis. However, the following three considerations should be looked at when choosing a standard:

- Fitness for purpose
- Reputation
- Existing experience

Fitness for purpose

- Is the proposed standard fit for its purpose?
- Does the structure it recommends makes sense for the documentation of the proposed resource?
- Are the categories of information it suggests to record relevant?
- Has it been used for similar resources before?

Some standards are geared to the description of museums information, others explicitly for visual arts resources, whereas others still are more generic and are used for all types of electronic resources or subject areas.

Reputation

How well established and widely used is it?

Standards receive varying degrees of acceptance and take-up within information communities. Try to choose ones with wide usage, organised control and that are well supported.

Existing experience

Does anyone in your organisation have any knowledge of using the standard(s) you are considering?

If so, this will reduce learning curves amongst project staff, or do you know of an associated organisation or colleague who has successfully used it who may be able to advise you on its implementation?

A succinct survey of relevant data documentation standards

This survey is based on the following document – Visual Arts, Museums and Cultural Heritage

Information Standards; A domain-specific review of relevant standards for networked information discovery (Gill, Grout, Smith – http://vads.ahds.ac.uk/standards.html), which provides a more comprehensive entry under each standard than is being made available herein. Three types of standards are described here. Those relating to:

- Networked resources generally
- The description of visual arts resources
- The description of museum information

1 General standards for networked resources

The Dublin Core
The Dublin Metadata Core Element Set, or Dublin Core, is a set of 15 descriptive elements used to provide a simple means of describing networked electronic information resources to aid more effective discovery and retrieval.

The Dublin Core is most commonly implemented by inserting the relevant descriptive information in the header of each web page that appears on the Internet. This greatly facilitates the retrieval of information on the Internet and can reduce the randomness of Internet searches

For more information about the Dublin Core, its implementation and a discussion of its relevance to the visual arts also see Section 4.3

IAFA templates
The IAFA templates were originally devised as a simple means to catalogue the contents of FTP archives.

There are a number of different types of IAFA templates, used for describing different types of resources. Most of the templates are used for describing individual files (documents, images, software package etc.), and use the same basic set of attribute (or field) values. There are also a number of templates for describing other types of resources, such as services, logical archives and mirrors.

Machine Readable Cataloguing (MARC)
MARC (ISO 2709/ANSI Z39.2) was first deployed in 1968, and is undoubtedly the oldest metadata format in existence. Originally developed as a standard data record structure detailing every aspect of the storage of bibliographic data (down to the specification of the physical tolerances of the magnetic tape it is stored on!), it has been modified over the years to provide a rich and flexible structure for the storage of a wide range of information types, including the description of digital resources (the 856 fields). The key benefits of MARC are derived from the fact that it is the standard bibliographic format for libraries around the world.

2 Specific standards for visual arts resources

Categories for the Description of Works of Art
Produced by the Art Information Task Force (AITF), the Categories for the Description of Works of Art are guidelines for formulating the content of art databases. They articulate an intellectual structure for descriptions of objects and image. In this sense they constitute a schematic representation of the requirements and assumptions implicit in the practice of the discipline of art history. By providing a single, encompassing, framework for descriptive

information about works of art, the Categories are intended to enhance compatibility between diverse systems that wish to share art information.

The Van Eyck Core Record
The Van Eyck project, which developed this standard, was driven by its art historical content rather than by the development of technology: the definition of a core record was at its heart. It is intended to provide a definition of the minimum fields needed to retrieve information about art images. It was arrived at by analysing the structure of several existing art image databases, including those of the project partners, and identifying the commonly occurring fields.

Visual Resources Association (VRA) Core Record
The VRA core group of data categories has been developed for describing surrogate images of art and architecture in visual resources collections and for sharing that information electronically. The core is a level between minimal and full and suggests which data elements are required in order to describe an item in a visual resources collection in a shared environment.

3 Specific standards for museums and cultural heritage information
CIDOC Standards
The Documentation Committee of the International Council of Museums (CIDOC) comprises a number of working groups whose work has resulted in standards publication. There are parallels to be drawn between such work and that of the AHDS in that there is, at one and the same time, domain-specific initiatives (e.g. archaeology, contemporary art) within a generic framework (e.g. the CIDOC Data Model).

SPECTRUM: the UK Museum Documentation Standard
As a procedural standard detailing the data needed for 20 collections management procedures, SPECTRUM was a world first. A 'cut-down' version, SPECTRUM Essentials, is available at the MDA web pages at http://www.open.gov.uk/mdocassn/mdase_00.htm

MDA Data Standard
Revised in 1991, this standard was originally developed in the 1960s, when it focused entirely on issues of cataloguing. It was extended in the 1980s to include some aspects of collections management, and in its latest edition consists of approximately 160 fields, which are categorised as being either Primary, Group or Common.

CIMI DTD
CIMI (the Consortium for the Computer Interchange of Museum Information) is a group of museums and museum bodies which have come together to further the cause of pooling and exchanging museum information. CIMI aims to make progress at both a theoretical and a practical level.

CIMI decided at an early stage in Project CHIO to use the SGML standard (Standard Generalized Markup Language; International Standard ISO 8879:1986) to mark up the textual resources involved in the project (exhibition catalogues and wall texts). In order to do this, it had to adopt or develop a Document Type Definition (DTD), a set of rules that defines the allowed structure of SGML documents. SGML requires that every valid document should have an associated DTD, and since no DTDs had been developed for museum information of any sort, it was decided that a new DTD was required.

SCRAN Data Standard
The SCRAN (Scottish Cultural Resources Access Network) Data Standard has defined 22 categories for use, cataloguing cultural resources which have been mapped to Dublin Core and SPECTRUM

Object ID
Object ID is a core standard for the identification of art, antiques and antiquities. It has been created as part of the Getty initiative to protect cultural objects and includes images among its categories. In the event of theft/loss Object ID is intended to allow the quick transmission of information about objects among museums, police and customs agencies, the art trade and collectors, (http://www.getty.edu/gri/standard/pco/).

SECTION 4.3 RESOURCE DISCOVERY METADATA AND THE DUBLIN CORE

As explained in the introduction to this section, there is nothing particularly mysterious about metadata, it simply means electronic data about electronic data. Sometimes the word is used very loosely and can be used to mean any kind of digital documentation about electronic resources. However, 'metadata' is most commonly used to refer to the descriptive information we provide about everything that exists on the Internet. (For a more general explanation about the Internet, HTML and how to create it see Section 8.2.)

The use of Dublin Core metadata is very important in this context as it could become the key to more effective retrieval of information via the Internet. When you carry out a search using one of the common search engines like Yahoo or AltaVista, what effectively takes place is a free text search of all the information contained on the Internet; it does not provide you with any indication prior to this search of the context in which your term appears.

Therefore, you may search for Auguste Renoir hoping to find information about the artist, his life and works, and come back with:

- hit 1. Auguste Renoir Hotel in Paris ***
- hit 2. Auguste Renoir Carmichael; Sportswear for all seasons
- hit 3. Auguste Renoir, for a color reproduction of the "Les Parapluies" $50, credit card transactions available

The use of Dublin Core metadata is intended to reduce the inherent randomness of searching for information about the chaotic global library presented via the Internet. Unwanted search results can be greatly reduced by introducing sensible and structured categories of information to describe networked resources, such as: a title, a name of author and resource description.

Dublin Core metadata is detected by a browser, by each 'parcel' of information being prefaced by the code 'dc'. The Dublin Core consists of 15 logical categories of information, called Elements, as follows:

(This definition has been taken from Dublin Core Metadata Element Set Reference Description, Version 1.1, 2nd July 1999: http://purl.org/dc/elements/1.1)

TITLE	The name given to the resource Comment: Typically, a Title will be a name by which the resource is formally known)
CREATOR	Definition: An entity primarily responsible for making the content of the resource Comment: Examples of a Creator include a person, an organisation, or a service. Typically the name of a creator should be used to indicate the entity
SUBJECT	Definition: The topic of the content of the resource Comment: Typically, a Subject will be expressed as keywords, key phrases or classification codes that describe a topic of the resource. Recommended best practice is to select a value from a controlled vocabulary or formal classification scheme.
DESCRIPTION	Definition: An account of the content of the resource Comment: Description may include but is not limited to: an abstract, table of contents, reference to a graphical representation of content or a free-text account of the content.
PUBLISHER	Definition: An entity responsible for making the resource available Comment: Examples of a Publisher include a person, an organisation, or a service. Typically, the name of a Publisher should be used to indicate the entity.
CONTRIBUTOR	Definition: An entity responsible for making contributions to the content of the resource. Comment: Examples of a Contributor include a person, an organisation, or a service. Typically, the name of a Contributor should be used to indicate the entity.
DATE	Definition: A date associated with an event in the life cycle of the resource. Comment: Typically, Date will be associated with the creation or availability of the resource. Recommended best practice for encoding the date value is defined in a profile of ISO 8601 [W3CDTF] and follows the YYYY-MM-DD format.
TYPE	Definition: The nature or genre of the content of the resource. Comment: Type includes terms describing general categories, functions, genres, or aggregation levels for content. Recommended best practice is to select a value from a controlled vocabulary (for example, the working draft list of Dublin Core Types [DCT1]). To describe the physical or digital manifestation of the resource, use the FORMAT element.
FORMAT	Definition: The physical or digital manifestation of the resource. Comment: Typically, Format may include the media-type or dimensions of the resource. Format may be used to determine the software, hardware or other equipment needed to display or operate the resource. Examples of dimensions include size and duration. Recommended best practice is to select a value from a controlled vocabulary (for example, the list of Internet Media Types [MIME] defining computer media formats).
IDENTIFIER	Definition: An unambiguous reference to the resource within a given context. Comment: Recommended best practice is to identify the resource by means of a string or number conforming to a formal identification system. Example formal identification systems include the Uniform Resource Identifier (URI) (including the Uniform Resource Locator (URL)), the Digital Object Identifier (DOI) and the International Standard Book Number (ISBN).
SOURCE	Definition: A Reference to a resource from which the present resource is derived. Comment: The present resource may be derived from the Source resource in whole or in part. Recommended best practice is to reference the resource by means of a string or number conforming to a formal identification system.

LANGUAGE	Definition: A language of the intellectual content of the resource. Comment: Recommended best practice for the values of the Language element is defined by RFC 1766 [RFC1766] which includes a two-letter Language Code (taken from the ISO 639 standard [ISO639]), followed optionally, by a two-letter Country Code (taken from the ISO 3166 standard [ISO3166]). For example, 'en' for English, 'fr' for French, or 'en-uk' for English used in the United Kingdom.
RELATION	Definition: A reference to a related resource. Comment: Recommended best practice is to reference the resource by means of a string or number conforming to a formal identification system.
COVERAGE	Definition: The extent or scope of the content of the resource. Comment: Coverage will typically include spatial location (a place name or geographic coordinates), temporal period (a period label, date, or date range) or jurisdiction (such as a named administrative entity). Recommended best practice is to select a value from a controlled vocabulary (for example, the Thesaurus of Geographic Names [TGN]) and that, where appropriate, named places or time periods be used in preference to numeric identifiers such as sets of coordinates or date ranges.
RIGHTS	Definition: Information about rights held in and over the resource. Comment: Typically, a Rights element will contain a rights management statement for the resource, or reference a service providing such information. Rights information often encompasses Intellectual Property Rights (IPR), Copyright, and various Property Rights. If the Rights element is absent, no assumptions can be made about the status of these and other rights with respect to the resource.

Table 3: Dublin Core Metadata Element Set descriptions

Qualifying Dublin Core

Dublin Core categories can also be *qualified* to provide a more specific spin on your descriptive information. For example, dc.date could logically become dc.date.created or dc.date.last-modified. Attempts have been made over the past three years to register a list of appropriate *qualifiers* internationally. However it is difficult to achieve a definitive list as many subject domains have invented their own qualifiers, many of which overlap with each other. It has also been mooted in a recent report that a distinction should be made between simple Dublin Core – simply dc, and qualified Dublin Core – dcq. This could allow metadata enabled search engines and other automated processes which may read or 'parse' metadata to know more definitively what they are encountering. An excellent update to the issues surrounding dc qualifiers and good practice recommendations for their implementation is found in Guidance on expressing the Dublin Core within the Resource Description Framework (RDF) (ed. Eric Miller, Paul Miller, Dan Brickley, July 1999) Section 3. *Enriching the Dublin Core* (http://www.ukoln.ac.uk/metadata/resources/dc/datamodel/WD-dc-rdf/)

It is possible to see how these qualifiers could be used in the implementation example given below.

Dublin Core Implementation Example

What follows is an example of Dublin Core metadata in action in the index page of the VADS website. As you can see, it is inserted in the header of the document before the main text or *body* of the document begins

```
<HEAD>
<TITLE>Visual Arts Data Service home page</TITLE>

<META NAME="description" CONTENT="Visual Arts Data Service">

<META NAME="DC.Description" CONTENT="(LANG = en) The home page for the Visual
Arts Data Service, A JISC-funded service to provide networked digital resources for the UK
higher education community in the visual arts. VADS also advises on standards of good
practice for the creation, description and preservation of digital information">

<META NAME="keywords" CONTENT="visual arts data service, vads, arts & humanities
data service, ahds, preservation">

<META NAME="DC.Title" CONTENT="Visual Arts Data Service">

<META NAME="DC.Subject" CONTENT="visual arts data service, vads, arts & humanities
data service, ahds, preservation">

<META NAME="DC.Author" CONTENT="(TYPE=homepage) http://vads.ahds.ac.uk/">

<META NAME="DC.Date.Created" CONTENT="(SCHEME = ISO 31–1) 1996–12–10">

<META NAME="DC.Date.LastModified" CONTENT="(SCHEME = ISO 31–1) 1998–01–
08">
<META NAME="DC.Format" CONTENT="(SCHEME=imt) text/html">

<META NAME="DC.Identifier" CONTENT="(TYPE=url) http://vads.ahds.ac.uk/">

<META NAME="DC.Relation.IsChildOf" CONTENT="(TYPE=childof) http://ahds.ac.uk">

<META NAME="DC.Rights" CONTENT="http://vads.ahds.ac.uk/Rights.html">

<META NAME="DC.Language" CONTENT="(SCHEME=iso639) en">

<META NAME="GENERATOR" CONTENT="Mozilla/3.03Gold (Win95; I) [Netscape]">
</HEAD>
<BODY>
```

The Edinburgh Workshop and its recommendations

In March 1997, The Visual Arts Data Service, in partnership with the Art, Design, Architecture
& Media Information Gateway, the Museum Documentation Association and the Scottish
Cultural Resources Access Network, held a workshop in Abden House Edinburgh to examine
the descriptive information needed to enable the discovery of visual arts, museums and cultural
heritage resources on the Internet, particularly in the form of digital images. This was part of
a series of five discipline-specific metadata workshops, organised by the Arts & Humanities

Data Service and the UK Office for Library Networking, with funding from the Joint Information Systems Committee of the Higher Education Funding Councils.

The workshop aimed to decide which DC descriptors were of 'core' significance, to indicate relevant specialist standards, terminology resources, syntaxes etc. and to consider the effectiveness of Dublin Core as a basis for resource discovery metadata in this domain.

This exercise was in some respects a complex one, as a very significant corpus of information description standards already exists for use by members of the three communities represented. A review of these standards was provided in a document circulated in advance for the participants (Gill, Grout, Smith -*Visual Arts, Museums & Cultural Heritage Information Standards*: http://vads.ahds.ac.uk/standards.html).

The workshop was followed by an extensive process of reporting and consultation in order both to recommend solutions to the problems identified at the workshop and to subject these recommendations to a process of rigorous review by members of the relevant communities. The reports which detail this process are available on the Visual Arts Data Service site on the World Wide Web (Gill and Grout 1997: *Visual Arts, Museums & Cultural Heritage Metadata Workshop Report* http://vads.ahds.ac.uk/metadataf1.html).

Recommendations
Identification of the source of intellectual content
One of the most significant problems the workshop addressed was the need to identify the source of intellectual content when creating and using resource discovery metadata. In essence the discussions at the workshop led to the need to find an effective answer to the following question:

How can a clear distinction between originals, surrogates, and on-line resources be made using Dublin Core?

The process of creating metadata about digital networked resources will often involve the description of a number of different entities since the investment of intellectual content can occur at many stages, e.g. at the creation and subsequent depiction/recording of a piece. Additionally, information in the visual arts, museum and cultural heritage fields is often derived from physical, tangible original objects such as works of art, objects in a collection, or sites of historic interest. Thus the ability to have the option to specify what exactly is being described by the metadata becomes more significant than for less object-focused research areas.

The principal solution proposed to this problem by the Visual Arts Data Service was the application of optional 'intellectual content source' qualifiers. These were:

* Original
* Surrogate
* Resource

These can be further refined by the use of the optional sub-qualifiers:

* Analogue
* Digital

NB: Whilst, these qualifiers could be applied to any of the Dublin Core's elements, they are too syntactically complex for widespread implementation and they could also represent a barrier to cross-domain searching.

Granularity: items and collections

The Dublin Core originated from the library community, and was originally intended to provide a simple means of describing document-like objects which were defined by example. Over the course of the Dublin Core workshop series, however, the element set was refined and the notion of a document-like object extended to include any networked resource that appears to be identical to diverse users. This means that the Dublin Core can now be used to describe a much wider range of networked resources.

This also paves the way for the application of the Dublin Core to descriptions at varying levels of granularity; it can still be used to describe a discrete individual item such as a Web page or a digital image, but it can also now be applied to more general resources, such as a collection of Web pages forming a site, or multiple digital images arranged as a collection.

This tension between *item* and *collection* level descriptions is particularly pertinent for the visual arts domain, as both the original works and the digital resources based upon them will tend to exist both as individual items and as parts of larger collections. Descriptions of both the items and the collections will inevitably be used for retrieval by users, depending upon their search goals.

The problem is further exacerbated by the fact that collections can be contained within larger collections. For example, a collection of objects donated by an individual may form part of the larger collection of a museum or gallery, but will still need to retain its unique identity and provenance.

VADS recommended the use of qualifiers for DC.relation, as suggested by members of the wider Dublin Core community. The most useful qualifier to allow relationships between items and collections was felt to be DC.relation.isMemberOf.

Need for user documentation and implementation guidelines

It was recommended during the course of the workshop that more information was needed to allow consistent interpretations and implementations of the Dublin Core. This was borne out by the experience of members of an editorial group elected at the workshop, who used the VADS' *Edinburgh Recommendations* as a basis for the construction of sample metadata on items from their collections.

Although a template was supplied, implementations still differed substantially between the authors, suggesting that domain-specific as well as general guidelines will be needed in future to allow for consistent resource description and discovery.

Need for wider awareness of the high-granularity resource discovery needs of this domain

Essentially, the workshop highlighted an issue at the heart of resource discovery requirements for visual arts, museums, and cultural heritage material. While the Dublin Core was invented to describe document-like objects, it is anticipated that members of these communities will wish to use the Core to describe and retrieve information about more complex and multilevel entities such as an electronic exhibition catalogue which could, for example, contain descriptions of the life and work of several artists, each accompanied by several digital images. Given the diverse and complex electronic resources which exist in this domain, it is therefore particularly important when using Dublin Core to define where the basis of intellectual content lies and what exactly the metadata is setting out to describe.

An example of an implementation of the Dublin Core in the Visual Arts

The example below shows how you could use Dublin Core to describe a website and the different elements within it. The website used here is for the Dickens House Museum, and the metadata is describing one particular page of the site, the introductory page.

When looking at this example it is worthwhile noting that it stretches the essentially simple structure of the Dublin Core to its very limits:

The assumption made in creating this metadata would be that the user would want to retrieve information, not only about the site and who created it, but about the different elements represented in it:

• The house depicted in the image on the page
• The architect of the depicted house
• The photograph of the house
• The digital image

(Some of the information contained in the example below is fictional.)

1st Page of Website (Title Page)

<META NAME=package.begin CONTENT="Dublin Core">

<!--Description of web site-->

<META NAME=dc.TITLE CONTENT = "(LANG=en) A Visit to the Dickens House">
<META NAME=dc.DESCRIPTION CONTENT = "(LANG=en) These web pages are based on the tour book available to those who can visit the actual Dickens House Museum. Neither the booklet nor these pages are any substitute for actually going to the museum. The site contains a summary of Dickens' life while living in the house and a description of the main content of each floor. ">
<META NAME=dc.SUBJECT CONTENT = "(SCHEME=AAT)(LANG=en) historic house museums, novels, illustrations, Victorian">
<META NAME=dc.SUBJECT CONTENT = "(LANG=en)Dickens, Charles">
<META NAME=dc.LANGUAGE CONTENT = "(SCHEME=ISO639) en">
<META NAME=dc.DATE CONTENT = "(SCHEME=ISO8601) 1996–05–01">

<META NAME=dc.PUBLISHER CONTENT = "(LANG=en) The Dickens Project, University of California, Santa Cruz">
<META NAME=dc.FORMAT CONTENT = "(SCHEME=IMT) text/html">
<META NAME=dc.IDENTIFIER CONTENT = "http://humwww.ucsc.edu/dickens/DEA/CDVE/Dickens.House/vist.to.house.html> <!—Information about photograph—> : Dickens Metadata Record Two>
<META NAME=dc.CREATOR.surrogate.analogue CONTENT = "(LANG=en) Jones, I">
<META NAME=dc.DESCRIPTION.surrogate.analogue CONTENT = "(LANG=en) Black & white photograph of Dickens' house at 48 Doughty Street.">

<!—Information about House in photo —>

<META NAME=dc.CREATOR.original.analogue CONTENT = "(LANG=en) Walsh, Hubert">

```
<META NAME=dc.CREATOR.original.analogue.birthDate CONTENT = "1789">
<META NAME=dc.CREATOR.original.analogue.deathDate CONTENT = "1823">
<META NAME=dc.DESCRIPTION.original.analogue CONTENT = "(LANG=en) House at
48 Doughty Street, London, occupied by Charles Dickens from 1837 to 1839.">
<META NAME=dc.SUBJECT.original.analogue.place.creation CONTENT = "(LANG=en)
London, England">
<META NAME=dc.SUBJECT.original.analogue.artType CONTENT =
"(SCHEME=AAT)(LANG=en) architecture">
<META NAME=dc.SUBJECT.original.analogue.Style CONTENT =
"(SCHEME=AAT)(LANG=en) Regency">
<META NAME=dc.SUBJECT.original.analogue.currentOwner CONTENT = "(LANG=en)
The Dickens House Museum Trust">
<META NAME=dc.DATE.original.analogue.creation CONTENT = "1818"
<!—Information about Digital Image —>
<META NAME=dc.TITLE.surrogate.digital CONTENT = "(LANG=en) dh.photo.gif">
<META NAME=dc.FORMAT.surrogate.digital CONTENT = "(SCHEME=IMT) image/gif">
<META NAME=dc.DATE.surrogate.digital.creation CONTENT = " SCHEME=ISO8601)
1996–05–01"

<META NAME=package.end CONTENT="Dublin Core"?
```

This lengthy example is actually an excerpt of the full example that was created for the Dickens House Website in order to test using Dublin Core to describe multi-level entities within websites.

VADS would not recommend that it is sensible to use Dublin Core to this extent in the headers of Internet documents, as it is extremely time consuming and complex to construct (even for the expert). It would also not necessarily be searchable even by those engines which have been tailored to retrieve on Dublin Core metadata.

However, it does stand as an interesting example of how the Core logically extends to embrace highly granular resources and moreover how it could be implemented in a visual arts, museums and cultural heritage context.

SECTION 4.4 TERMINOLOGY RESOURCES AND CLASSIFICATION SCHEMES

Terminology resources and classification schemes provide for the structured creation and fully enabled retrieval of datasets. This section gives an introduction to an important and useful selection of these tools, which can greatly enhance electronic resources created for the visual arts.

Terminology resources

These act as 'control vocabularies' which remove the idiosyncrasies of cataloguing and thereby enhance information retrieval. They ensure that when disparate cataloguers approach similar items, the terms they use are either exactly the same or are linked to compatible ones. This is especially necessary within the international and culturally fluid arena of visual arts data.

However, it is also worth noting that terminology resources also have the advantage of allowing diverse systems to inter-operate better with one another. Applying them to your collection records will hence expand the usage-horizons of your data.

Much work in this area is carried out by The Getty Research Institute's Vocabulary Program (http://www.getty.edu/gri/vocabularies/index.htm). This includes:

- The Union List of Artist Names (ULAN)
- The Art and Architecture Thesaurus (AAT)
- The Getty Thesaurus of Geographic Names (TGN).

Union List of Artist Names

Having a standard list of artists' names is a clear asset to the process of creating good visual arts documentation – the whole process of searching for and retrieving information falls down very easily if artists are not referred to consistently. Confusion can arise as historical, cultural and regional variants do exist, and have certainly been used in the creation of documentation about many artists.

ULAN features

- 200,000+ names, identifying approximately 100,000 individual artists, or 'creators'
- Wide subject coverage, including:
  Fine artists
  Performance artists
  Decorative artists
  Architects
- 'Clustered' data format
- Bibliographic citations

Advantages

The ULAN clustered format links all of the data relating to a particular creator in a single record. For example, in the cluster for which the Entry Form is Giambologna (Jean Boulogne), the artist's nationality appears as both Flemish and Italian; his roles are listed by different contributors as architect, sculptor, mannerist sculptor, and goldsmith; and birth-dates of 1529 and c.1524 are given.

This is a departure from the orthodox notion of an authority file, but reflects the fact that in the field of art history there isn't always a single correct answer. A ULAN record can thus also serve as a mini critical history of an artist or architect.

This 'mini-history' asset is enhanced by the inclusion of bibliographic citations. These improve the efficiency and the economy of: building authority files, indexing art-related materials and retrieving information on artists.

Example

Below is an abbreviated search result from ULAN. (The full record contains over 75 variant names that have been used to denote *Caravaggio*. The list below suggests the evident confusions that can arise when one artist is given a name commonly associated with another, in this case Michelangelo.)

Caravaggio, Michelangelo Merisi da
(Italian painter, 1573–1610)

>   Caravaggio, Michelangelo Merisi (wrongly Merigi, Amerigi or Amerighi) da
>   Michelangelo
>   Michelangelo Amerighi da Caravaggio
>   Michelangelo Caravaggi
>   Michel'Angelo Caravaggio
>   Michelangelo Caravagli
>   Michelangelo da Caravaccio
>   Michel'Angelo da Caravaggio
>   Michelangelo da Caravaggio
>   Michelangelo Garavaggi
>   Michelangelo Merisi, called Caravaggio
>   Michelangelo Merisi da Caravaggio

ULAN is available to search on the web at:
http://shiva.pub.getty.edu/ulan_browser/

Art and Architecture Thesaurus

The AAT is a controlled vocabulary that embraces all the different words which we may wish to use when documenting visual arts resources. It has effectively established a controlled dictionary of terms which can be used to standardise and add quality control and consistency to the process of cataloguing. The vocabulary contained within the AAT is extremely powerful and wide ranging.

AAT Features

- 120,000+ terms for describing the visual arts architecture and material culture, including:
    Material and techniques
    Physical attributes
    Historical, critical and theoretical context
    Function and purpose
- Time span from antiquity to the present.
- Main focus is on the Western world but it does embrace other cultures as well

At the first level of the hierarchy within the thesaurus, the AAT has been divided into seven subjects or groupings:

1   Associated Concepts
2   Physical Attributes
3   Styles and Periods
4   Agents
5   Activities
6   Materials
7   Objects.

These are further divided into 33 subheadings. A preferred term is established for each concept which is known as a 'descriptor'. Other or alternative terms are also given with this. This whole powerful system is enhanced by the addition of relationships which link up related concepts into a meaningful structure. This network or 'map' between concepts can operate as a means of searching databases of art information.

Because of the richness of this vocabulary the Getty Research Institute sees it as being of relevance for use by all of the following groupings:
archives and special collections, libraries, museums, visual resources collections, conservation agencies

It is possible to access the AAT on the web at
http://shiva.pub.getty.edu/aat_browser/

Example
To give an indication of the kind of results it is possible to obtain, below is sample search result on the word Mezzotint

> **AAT Term Information**
> Descriptor: **mezzotint**
> Hierarchy: **Processes and Techniques [KT]**

Scope note – **Intaglio process in which the surface of the plate is methodically roughened with a rocker to produce a dark background; areas may then be lightened using various scrapers. Produces a printed image having a continuous tonal range. PRTT**

> Synonyms and spelling variants {UF}:
> **black manner**
> **engraving, mezzotint**
> **manière anglaise**
> **manière noire**
> **manner, black**
> **mezzotint engraving**

> You may also be interested in the following related concepts {RT}
> **mezzotints**
> **mezzotinters**

Getty Thesaurus of Geographic Names (TGN)
The Getty TGN is a structured vocabulary developed primarily for the field of art history. It also has the potential for wider applications in related disciplines such as archaeology, history and geography. Geographic names from the thesaurus can be used to record:

- The current location of an art object
- Place of origin
- The loci of activity of an artist
- The sites of an artist's birth and death.

The TGN is the only available geographical resource that is both hierarchical and global in scope.

TGN features

- Approx. 1 million place names representing 900,000 places
- Historically/Internationally/Culturally sensitive
- Physical and political entities represented
- Place types defined

Place attributes

Each place has 'attributes', including names, place types and coordinates. The places are arranged in hierarchies representing the current political and physical world and historical places are being added.

Each name is followed by two capital letters, or 'flags', in parentheses. These indicate the following:

- for current name
- H for historical name
- V for vernacular name
- O for a variant name in a language other than the vernacular

Places in the TGN can be either physical or political entities. Physical entities include continents, rivers, and mountains. Political entities include: empires, nations, states, districts, townships, cities, and neighbourhoods.

'Place Type' is a term that describes a significant aspect of the place, including: its role, function, political anatomy, size, or physical characteristics. Place types are indexing terms chosen from the structured vocabulary of the AAT. As is true of names, place types are also ordered logically and may have associated display dates.

Example

A search of TGN on Nice yielded several results, including the following:

Nice........(inhabited place)

    (Europe, France, Provence-Alpes-Côte d'Azur, Alpes-Maritimes) [7008773]

It was then selected for further investigation. The richness and complexity of the information available is clearly demonstrated in the example that follows

[7008773]

Nice (inhabited place)

Lat: **43 42 N** Long: **007 16 E**

Note – **Conquered by Romans 1st cen. AD; ruled by Saracens 10th cen.; under counts of Savoy 1388–1860, although captured and held by French several times; pillaged by Turks 1543; ceded to France 1860; birthplace of Garibaldi; leading resort city of French Riviera.**

Hierarchical Position:

      Europe........(continent)

        France.....(nation)

           Provence-Alpes-Côte d'Azur..(region)

             Alpes-Maritimes...(department)

Names:

Nice (C,V)
Nizza (C,O)
Nicaea (H,O)........ ancient
Nicea Liguriae (H,O)
Nikaia (H,O)

Place Types:

inhabited place (C).......
founded by Phocaeans from ancient Massilia (Marseille), 350 BC city (C)
department capital (C)
port (C)
trade center (C)......
since ancient Roman times, 1st cen. AD
tourist center (C)
resort (C)

Sources:

Nicaea.... Webster's Geographical Dictionary (1984) [FDA]

Nice....... Columbia Lippincott Gazetteer (1961) [BHA] Columbia Lippincott
Gazetteer (1961) [GCPS] Michel: Dictionnaire des Communes (1984) [BHA] Webster̂s
Geographical Dictionary (1984) [FDA] Times Atlas of the World (1994), 139 [VP]
Encyclopædia Britannica (1988), VIII, 677 [VP] Webster's Geographical Dictionary (1988),
846 [VP]
Nicea Liguriae.. ARLIS/NA: Ancient Site Names (1995) [VP]
Nikaia...... ARLIS/NA: Ancient Site Names (1995) [VP]

Nizza.... Columbia Lippincott Gazetteer (1961) [GCPS] Webster's
Geographical Dictionary (1984) [FDA]
You can search the TGN on the web at
http://shiva.pub.getty.edu/tgn_browser/

Classification schemes
ICONCLASS (http://iconclass.let.uu.nl/)
ICONCLASS is a hierarchical alphanumeric classification system for the indexing and
organisation of the visual content or 'iconographŷs2 of art works and their surrogate images.
Thus it deals with the pictorial image itself, rather than information about the work or the artist.
Developed in The Netherlands by H. van de Waal but published in English, ICONCLASS has
been deployed in many European and American museums, slide libraries, photographic archives
and documentation centres. It is used extensively in the Witt Index at the Courtauld Institute of
Art.
    The basis of ICONCLASS is the notion that the subject of a work of art can be made up of
a combination of people, events, situations, objects and also ideas. ICONCLASS stemmed

from the idea that it would be useful and possible to create a classification scheme based on the identification and coding of these diverse entities relevant to the subject of a given work.

Each concept is given a place in a hierarchy and accorded an accompanying alpha numeric notation.

The top level of the hierarchy is as follows

0   Abstract, Non-representational Art
1   Religion and Magic
2   Nature
3   Human being, Man in general
4   Society, Civilization, Culture
5   Abstract Ideas and Concepts
6   History
7   Bible
8   Literature
9   Classical Mythology and Ancient History

These are designed to represent all the general categories into which the subject of an image could be divided.

ICONOCLASS is provided in printed and electronic forms. The advantage of a classification system over controlled vocabulary for image documentation is that it is independent of language, bans internal ambiguity and is arranged in a transparent hierarchy.

Applying this system to a visual resource would enable retrieval on direct visual content, rather than textual descriptions of the work. Thus motifs could be searched for irrespective of media or their pre-eminence in a work etc.

Resource terminology and multilinguality

Multilinguality is of prime concern to visual arts resource professionals; below is a brief survey of recent work focused in this area:

- CHIN is undertaking French equivalency work of the AAT
- The Escuela Tecnica Superior de Arquitectura, Universidad Politecnica de Madrid is doing the same in Spanish.
- The Multilingual Thesaurus of Religious objects based on Suppellettile ecclesiastic, published by ICCD
- Religious Objects/Objets religieux, published by the Canada/France Accord.
- The MDA is in the process of co-ordinating a project proposal to the EC for a feasibility project on multilingual terminology resources. TERM-IT (http://www.mda.org.uk/term-it/)
- A project to translate ICONCLASS (see above) into Italian is being undertaken by the Istituto Centrale per il Catalogo e la Documentazione (ICCD). Information can be found on the ICCD web site at http://www.iccd.beniculturali.it.
- The International Terminology Working Group at the Getty Research Institute have published guidelines for forming language equivalents. http://w.getty.edu/gri/

Section 5: Project and Collections Management

5.1 PROJECT MANAGEMENT

Introduction

Digital resource creation, under whatever circumstances, is best thought of as a *project*. There will be aims and objectives to define and meet, specifications to decide upon and resources to work within. Project management is thus an important area to be familiar with and have knowledge of for both planning and undertaking resource creation. Collections management is more specifically aimed at organising digital objects, once created.

There are a multitude of resources available related to project and collections management on a generic basis. This section introduces some of the management issues that are specific to creating digital resources.

The section considers both the *processes* involved in resource creation and the *tools* required to manage digital resources.

Project management
Introduction
While it is not suggested that a full-scale adoption of the project management techniques, tools and processes described in this section is appropriate for smaller-scale digital resource creation activities, they may be usefully applied to a wide range of data creation scenarios. They are particularly applicable to projects which involve the creation, management and delivery of a large number of digital records; for example a collection of digital images. This section also promotes awareness about what is distinct about a digital resource and its *life cycle* and how in some respects it requires special treatment differentiating it from the products or resources generated by non-digital projects.

Communication skills
A defining feature of good project management is effective communication between the various people involved in the project, and management of the relationships between the various activities or work packages involved in the process. As Kenney and Chapman state, in *Digital Imaging for Libraries and Archives, Department of Preservation and Conservation*, Cornell University Library, 1996: 'Successful project management recognises the interrelationship among each of the various processes, and appreciates that the decisions made at the beginning affect all subsequent steps'.

This is certainly true of the process of managing digital resource creation, where decisions made at the beginning of the digitisation process can radically affect the ultimate outcome. For example, decisions about the resolution that images are scanned at, or about how they are documented, though not always irreversible, will often dictate how the resource is delivered, used and ultimately what kind of useful lifespan it may have.

A 'Helicopter Viewpoint'

It is also important to note that effective project management is about maintaining a sense of perspective. Good project management will not lose sight of the whole picture, for example the external as well as internal forces that direct the digitisation process, and will not allow the minutiae of day-to-day problem solving to conceal the process of attaining final goals and objectives. At the same time the need for attention to detail must not be overlooked, and measures must be put into place early on to ensure that standards and quality of output is not allowed to slip (see Section 5.3 Quality Assurance).

Flexibility and responsiveness

Another important feature of successful project management in the digital arena is the ability to be flexible in changed circumstances, and to respond positively to criticism and feedback and act accordingly. In this time of rapid technological change and also changing levels of interest in and understanding of the use of digital resources by end users, it is this responsiveness and flexibility which will ultimately result in usable and sustainable digital resources.

Relevant experience

Effective and responsive leadership is required for project management. Thus a good overall understanding of all the issues involved is needed. It is important to note that while a 'project manager' may not necessarily need to possess in-depth knowledge and practical experience of all the technical issues involved, it is crucial that the manager is sufficiently technically literate to be able to liaise effectively with technically qualified team members, or other sources of technical support who possess detailed understanding of these issues.

Depending on the size of the project and resources available, some projects may only be able to house a skeletal staff, meaning that certain activities, for example digitisation or database design, may be reasonably out-sourced. In these cases it is important that the 'project manager' is aware of the overheads in terms of time and level of organisation that managing the work of external parties will incur.

It is also the case with smaller initiatives that the 'project manager' may reasonably combine management with implementing some of the other aspects of the process, for example copyright clearance, quality assurance or providing advice to users. However, even if project management as a specific activity cannot be justified within budget as a full-time post for one person, it is useful to allocate this role to a particular individual as a distinct function.

Project managing the digital resource life cycle: the 'seven ages' of a resource

As has already been stated, it is important to bear in mind that the stages below do not present a simple linear progression. Effective management is about bearing in mind all these elements, and respecting the inter-relationships between them. As has also been suggested, a flexible approach is needed so that planning and re-planning can take place throughout the data creation process. The following diagram shows the relationship between project implementation and planning

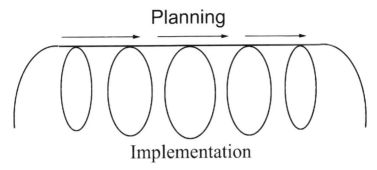

Figure 3: The relationship between project implementation and planning

The 'seven ages' of a digital resource

- Project planning
- Preparation for data creation
- Workflow and collections management
- Dissemination and collaboration
- Resource delivery
- User access and support
- Archiving and preservation

1 Project planning

Before embarking on any data creation exercise it is important to develop a *project plan* to help manage the process. (If external funding was applied for in order to commence a project involving data creation, a project plan may already have been created to provide evidence of detailed thought into how a project will be implemented.)

The project plan

A project plan will normally consist of a time line, indicating the main activities that will take place and their start and end dates. It may also usefully identify staff/organisations responsible for each activity.

Some tasks will have dependencies or direct relationships with other tasks, which the plan may also need to indicate. For example, you may not be able to commence digitisation until rights have been cleared, or you may not be able to make a resource live until appropriate quality testing has been done.

A project plan should not be a rod for your back but rather a source of useful guidance and an incentive to meet deadlines. It is also extremely rare that a project plan will not be updated to take account of unforeseen circumstances.

Software which can be easily edited is available to generate project plans, for example Microsoft Project (further details below).

Recruitment and staff management

This is in some respects self explanatory. However it is worth emphasising that the effort and time involved in recruiting, managing, motivating and retaining staff on the part of the project manager should not be under-estimated.

Budgetary management and forecasting
It is important to forecast projected expenditure and likely costs incurred as far ahead as possible, so that the budget is not merely a record of costs incurred but a method of safeguarding and future proofing the project.

This area may also involve generating preliminary exploitation plans for projects which have commercial potential to be developed, or to recover recurrent costs to allow the digital resource is to be maintained and updated in the future.

2 Preparation for data creation
Before digitisation commences a number of activities will need to take place, which will obviously differ in scale and complexity depending on the resource that is being created. Many of the areas covered here are dealt with in more detail in other areas of this Guide.

- Preparation of materials for digitisation – trialing data creation techniques and assimilating materials (see Section 3.7 for preparation for image creation)
- Establishing Rights Management framework – this will include a copyright clearance strategy and establishing procedures for licensing materials for your use as applicable (see Section 2.8)
- Purchasing and setting up equipment – this will include a production system, storage and backup media which should also be chosen with a view to future resource delivery and preservation (see Section 3 and section on Database creation and design)
- Selecting data documentation standards and controlled vocabularies to be used (see Section 4.)
- Selecting technical formats and standards to be used (Section 3 and Section 6.4)

3 Workflow and collections management
Ensuring a carefully planned workflow with effective and consistent project management is a clear priority for any digitisation initiative. The various elements of this are as follows:

- Designing and implementing a strategy for workflow – it will need to be considered how the various elements of your digitisation chain, from scanning originals to adding descriptive information to validating and enhancing data etc, best relate to each other and how this chain should be staffed and organised (see Section 5.2)
- Targets for content creation – these targets will allow progress to be tracked and should provide reassurance rather than unrealistic demands
- Quality control and assurance methods – these are the essential error and data integrity checks which help guarantee the quality of the resource being developed (see Section 5.3)
- Evaluation – time for reflection and self-evaluation is never wasted. It may be important to involve intended users in the evaluation of resource creation. (See Section 6.1 for resource delivery and user issues.)

4 Dissemination and collaboration
Ensuring that a digitisation project is not developed in isolation will help to guarantee its success. Therefore, particularly for larger initiatives, the following strategies are recommended:

- Develop links with key collaborators, to learn and share effort – there will probably be others involved in similar projects with whom fruitful relationships can be built
- Implement information channels – it is recommended to establish a website, JISCmail list and publicity leaflets to raise the resources profile among the intended user community and to request formative input
- Attend key dissemination events and conferences for presentations – this is again a good way of learning, sharing experiences and developing the profile of a data creation initiative (For more detailed information on these issues see Section 6.5)

5 Resource delivery

Once a resource is complete, some means of allowing the intended users access to it will be necessary. It is anticipated that the method or methods of resource delivery were selected at an early stage in the project to ensure that the standards and technologies selected are appropriate for the intended methods of disclosure. (NB the delivery system may result from a separate creation/tender process.)

The following are the main factors involved in implementing aspects of a resource delivery system:

- Implementing resource delivery method selected – for example Intranet, Internet, CD ROM etc. or interface with existing library or other in-house catalogue for example (see Section 6.1)
- Designing user interface or access layer – the appearance and design of this is crucial as it will define how, and indeed if, users can make effective use of the digital data created (see Section 6.2)
- User authentication process and resource ordering system – it may be desirable to restrict usage of data to particular 'classes of users', i.e. to higher education or non-profit making organisations etc. Therefore the delivery system may need to be able to recognise 'authorised' users, issue them with passwords, and potentially order data from the resource for individual use (see Section 6.3)
- Implementing protocols for information interchange – a common approach at present, which offers considerable benefits to users, is implementing a system where data can be exchanged with other data in a single query environment. Some examples of standards which allow information to be exchanged between different resources are Z39.50 and its profiles, and ensuring compliance with the Dublin Core. The latter is an international standard for describing networked resources like those on the Internet (see Section 6.4)
- System trialing, evaluation and enhancement – a great deal of time and effort may end up being spent on trying out and tweaking a system before users are allowed access to it. The time this may take should not be under-estimated in the project plan

6 User access and support

Once digital content is created and the means to deliver it to its intended audience is available, the priority is likely to be ensuring the resource is used as intended. This may involve the following activities:

- Dissemination and publicity – presenting completed data to the target community(ies)
- Developing a training and workshop program – it is necessary to bear in mind well in

advance how users will engage with a resource and to what extent training in the resource's use may be needed, particularly for the less computer literate

- Providing a help desk – for example responding to enquiries about data use, trouble shooting, administering orders for data and post-delivery support if relevant
- Implementing exploitation plans – to market the resource to end-users. if applicable (For more detailed information on these issues see Section 6.5.)

7 Archiving and preservation

An archiving and preservation strategy is particularly important for digital data as it is vulnerable to loss, decay of media and obsolescence of chosen formats, hardware and software. Resources which are dependent upon a specific hardware and software environment are particularly vulnerable. (See Section 7 for more guidelines on Digital Preservation.)

The investments made in creating data will be best justified and maximised by incorporating a preservation strategy into any original project plan.

Archiving and funding

The Visual Arts Data Service and Technical Advisory Service for Images, advise those developing a digital resource to include costs for preservation and archiving in any initial funding proposal itself.

Many funding councils that provide funds for digitisation also recognise that preservation and archiving should be a separately costed activity and increasingly require provision to be made for this activity.

Third party preservation and archiving

Digital archiving and preservation techniques are technically complex and resource-intensive activities requiring specialist skills and equipment. It is unlikely that 'deep storage' and technical preservation methods, which data archives are increasingly able to supply for the data in their care, will be available 'locally' to a resource.

Therefore, in general, rather than attempting to undertake these on an individual basis it is recommended these activities are contracted to a specialised third party, for both economies of scale and 'safety-net' provision.

Placing a copy of data in a recognised data archive, such as that provided by VADS for visual arts resources, is a recommended viable long-term preservation strategy.

(See Section 9.2 for further information on archiving)

Project management tools and courses

Tools

A commonly used suite of tools for project management are those supplied by Microsoft. Some of these come as a component of the MS Office software, included with many new PCs on purchase. The MS Office tools which are most applicable to project management are:

- *Microsoft Project* – to produce project plans
- *MS Access* – useful for building databases from scratch, for example a database could contain names and addresses of contacts for the project
- *Microsoft Excel* – to develop spreadsheets for budgetary management

- *Microsoft PowerPoint* – to produce materials for presentations
- *Microsoft Word* – for document production

For product information from Microsoft see http://www.microsoft.com/office/details.htm

It is often useful to use this suite of tools together, as information may then be readily cut and pasted between the various applications, thus avoiding duplication and helping to make the management process streamlined and consistent.

Equivalent MS Office tools are now also available for the Macintosh, see http://www.microsoft.com/macoffice/default.asp

Apple also supplies software tools which are useful for project management. These are AppleWorks, formerly ClarisWorks, which provide word processing, graphics and illustration, spreadsheet, charting/graphing, presentations and database capabilities. For product information, see http://w.apple.com/appleworks/.

If you are part of the UK higher education community you may find that these tools and other relevant software packages are available at a reduced rate through CHEST, see http://w.chest.ac.uk/software/tableindex.html – this page also contains product evaluations.

Courses

There are many commercially run courses on project management, some of which lead to accreditation by the Association for Project Management; for example those run by Cap Gemini (http://w.w.capgemini.co.uk/so/e&t_index.htm).

The web pages for the UK Association for Project Management provide a list of accredited courses http://www.apmgroup.co.uk/accours.htm.

Increasingly, however, members of the higher education, museums and archival and library community are offering project management training courses which are more specifically geared to managing data creation projects, for example the *'Introduction to management skills'* workshop on 20 and 21 September, in London, run by the Library Association (http://w.w.la-hq.org.uk/index.html).

Some courses are specifically concerned with managing information delivered via the Internet, for example those run by Netskills, see http://www.netskills.ac.uk/workshops/descriptions/man-info.html.

While courses on digital project management run from this sector are relatively new, it is likely that they will develop and multiply as a response to the rapid growth in the number of data creation projects and a recognition that effective management is directly benefited by specialist training.

5.2 WORKFLOW AND PROCEDURES MANAGEMENT

This section considers workflow and procedures management for creating a digital resource.

The building of a digital resource is a complex process but it should, with careful planning and consideration at the outset, prove to be a straightforward process. To help define each stage and the decisions to be made it is useful to determine the *workflow* of the project throughout the *whole digitisation chain.*

Consultation with all interested parties is recommended at this 'production planning' stage. Interested parties may include those responsible for:

- The analogue items
- Project management
- Rights management
- Digitisation
- Metadata structuring and input
- Delivery and user support services
- Archiving
- Quality assurance
- Evaluation

Depending on the size and nature of the project, these tasks may fall wholly or partly to individuals within the same organisation or to distinct organisations.

Resource creation phases

The phases of the workflow will include the following:

- Planning
- Assessing analogue items to be digitised
- Rights management
- Digitisation feasibility study – to determine digitisation procedures and benchmarks
- Digitisation – creating primary capture files and surrogate forms
- Adding metadata (technical and subject-based)
- Archiving
- Delivery
- Resource support
- Quality assurance
- Final evaluation

A careful consideration of the workflow will determine the following, for each phase:

- Operational specifications
- Targets for content creation
- Metadata requirements
- Any additional project management functions that are required from software (e.g. see Section 5.4 on database systems)
- QA provision (see Section 5.3)

These findings can be written up into a workflow or production plan document. This document can then form the basis of standard operating procedures which control each step.

Standard operating procedures need not be restrictive or set in stone, but should act as a firm guide. They can be refined with practice and over time.

Similarly, targets for content creation allow progress to be tracked, rather than the whip to be cracked. Targets should provide reassurances rather than unrealistic demands.

Procedures and strategies will need to be determined for each of the project's activities and these will require good management of workloads.

Both management of workloads and 'target setting' is aided by the inclusion of 'time and motion' analysis into any feasibility studies undertaken, e.g. prior to the full digitisation phase.

An important step to add at the end of the resource creation work flow is final evaluation. Following completion of a project it is beneficial to report on experiences, outcomes, findings and achievements. This may usefully include a survey of resource users' experiences with the delivered resource.

5.3 QUALITY ASSURANCE (QA)

QA is key to providing digital resources of a consistently high quality that meet the aims of a project. QA is a part of project management and can itself be an intensive undertaking. Its degree of application and formalisation, should be assessed according to the nature of particular digitisation projects: their size and aims.

QA is achieved by having agreed targets, recording mechanisms and quality checks, relevant to each phase of digitisation, planned for and in place throughout the resource's production.

For example, during the entering of metadata into a database to contextualise digital images, QA elements could include:

- Predefining the data entry options by the establishment of 'pull-down' menus under each field name
- Having a minimum set of metadata records, i.e. fields which cannot be left blank before 'saving' a record
- Attaching controlled vocabularies
- Having procedures in place for checking all entries for consistency and correctness vis a vis the digital object they describe

Such measures, would combine to alleviate operator interpretation and data-entry errors and ensure that 'like spellings' and alternative names etc. are automatically accounted for. (See Section 4 for metadata standards and controlled vocabularies for the visual arts and Section 5.4 for further information on database management systems.)

For QA procedures relevant to the capture of digital images see Section 3.7 . The TASI web-site also carries a Quality Assurance section specific to digital images, at: http://www.tasi.ac.uk/building/qa1.html

It is worth noting that QA issues should be considered not only from the perspective of the resource creators, but of other 'stakeholders' in the resource. These include:

- Rights holders
- Creators of original objects
- Subject experts
- End users

These are not necessarily mutually exclusive categories and it may be that any number of them coincide with the data creator. However if they are distinct bodies, it will be necessary to gain their insight into the acceptable end quality required from the digitisation exercise. This will provide the necessary 'benchmarks' from which the QA methods required to achieve those ends can be formulated.

5.4 DATABASE MANAGEMENT SYSTEMS

Introduction

A database is a highly effective tool for 'collections management' of a resource. A database can hold, structure and provide access to digital data created. A database can include both the digital objects themselves and their accompanying textual metadata, or provide a link between the two. Most visibly applied to 'image-base' type resources, databases feature at the 'back-end' of most digital content creation.

Database management systems

Most database software available provides more than simple organisation of data and hence it is useful to think of databases as potential management systems.

A database management system keeps a whole collection together and maintains the relationships between the digital objects created and their associated text or metadata. It provides a way to gather together all the relevant information and to store and maintain that information in a central place.

Depending on how complex a project is, the database can also be used to manage digitisation workflow and procedures. For example, a project may involve several digitisers and cataloguers. The database system can be used to manage workflow, provide quality assurance and administration tools, and keep track of key 'milestones'. (See project management, workflow and quality assurance, sections 5.1, 5.2, 5.3)

Issues in selecting a database system

No one database system is right for every situation and there are many different scenarios. The following are some issues which should be considered:

- Is the database being used to house the metadata and maintain the relationship between metadata and object?
- Is the database being used to manage workflow and production schedules?
- Does the project involve multiple users across different sites?
- What platforms need to be supported?
- Is the same system to be used to create, manage and deliver the collection?

Answers to these questions will result in the production of an operational specification and data model. The data model will define what data will be captured and how it is organised.

Types of database management systems

As with image manipulation software, there is a huge variety of database management systems available. These fall into broad categories which correspond to successive stages in the history of database theory, and provide a wide range of choices. In general, there is a trade-off between simplicity and flexibility: simpler systems which appear easy to use may, in the end, prove inflexible and result in a poorly structured and hard to maintain database.

The 'ease of use' of a particular database should only be considered within the context of a particular project's needs: the same database may be a joy to use for one task, but inappropriate for another.

Database systems can be categorised as:

- Flat file or table
- Relational (SQL)
- Object-oriented

Flat file or table

Flat-file systems are conceptually the simplest architecture, where the database is structured using a single table with one set of fields, much the same as a 'card-file' record. This can be useful, particularly for small databases, but may introduce redundancy (repetition) into records. For example, multiple images may have a single 'creator'; with flat-table systems, this information has to be entered separately for each image record. Relational databases were invented to solve precisely this problem.

Relational databases

The relational model establishes separate tables for each kind of entity in the database (e.g. Creator, Creation date, Image), and allows for the specification of relationships between data-tables. Together with Structured Query Language (SQL), the relational model is the current 'mainstream' approach to database architecture. Examples of packages include:

- Oracle
  (http://www.oracle.com/products/)
- MS Access
  (http://www.microsoft.com/office/access/default.asp)
- Claris Filemakerpro
  (http://w.filemaker.com/products/filemakerpro/filemakerpro.html)
- dBase
  (http://www.dbase2000.com/)
- mySQL
  (http://w.w.tcx.se/)
- MS SQL Server
  (http://w.microsoft.com/sql/default2.htm)

Object-oriented

Object-oriented (OO) databases are considered the 'next generation' of database technology and introduce still further expressiveness (and complexity), by representing an entity in the database as a complex object. This type of database has the concept of 'inheritance', where one type of object can be a sub-type of another type of object. OO databases are of particular relevance for *digital imaging projects*, due to the complex and hierarchically structured nature of the information being stored. Although OO databases are a relatively recent development, they are worth considering in cases where the relational model proves too rigid and inflexible.

Within these types of databases, there are various sub-categories and hybrids, most noticeably object-relational models, for example PostgreSQL.(http://w.pgsql.com)

Text mark-up approaches

An alternative approach to the storage of textual data is to use a markup language such as

SGML (Structured Generalised Markup Language) or its simplified subtext XML (eXtensible Markup Language). For image metadata purposes, XML is likely to be more than adequate and the additional power of SGML is unlikely to be required.

XML

XML is designed to allow communities of expertise to define their own document types and thus can be used by a wide variety of applications. The World Wide Web Consortium's (W3C) new Resource Development Framework (RDF) is an application of XML and will provide rich facilities for describing images and other resources using XML.

With the development of XML, two possible approaches to managing image metadata become feasible. Metadata about a resource could be marked up in XML and stored in either an XML document repository (see SIL resources page at http://www.sil.irg/SGML) or within the image itself.

Indexing and searching of RDF data expressed in XML is best considered a distinct issue from generic XML query. Although RDF is an application of XML, in that XML syntax is used to store and exchange RDF data, it is important to realise that XML (and SGML) storage and query systems are not well suited for use with RDF.

RDF is concerned with the logical structure of the data rather than the way in which fragments of that data happen to be stored. These issues are discussed in more detail in the position paper 'Enabling Inferencing' available from http://purl.org/net/rdf/papers/.

Object-oriented databases offer many facilities that are well suited to the storage of complex RDF metadata.

Database design

This section is largely derived from the work of Kenney and Chapman, 1996, *Digital Imaging for Libraries and Archives*, Department of Preservation and Conservation, Cornell University Library.

Good database design is essential to the usefulness of a database. The design will impose a structure that will establish the ways in which the database can be accessed and searched.

Database design should include the following elements:

- Controlled vocabulary
- Generality
- Simplicity

Controlled vocabulary

A controlled vocabulary allows field entries to be input from a pre-defined set of values (often through a 'pull-down menu' or 'pick-list'). This is an alternative to 'free text' data entry into fields, which can result in operator error (e.g. mis-spellings), being incorporated in the data. Any such input errors will hamper information retrieval. Using controlled vocabularies ensures against erroneous data entry and aids effective search functions.

A controlled vocabulary can be created by a project; that is, a set of common terms can be defined for use as field values. It will then be necessary to determine which terms (if not all) can be used to correlate with the objects within a database. A useful alternative or additional measure is to employ existing thesauri for these purposes. For more information about controlled vocabularies specific to the visual arts see Section 4.4.

Controlled vocabularies make databases more manageable for both data entry staff, who have set values to select from, and search interface designers who can use controlled search options against specific fields. This in turn benefits users by allowing quicker and directly correlated searching.

Generality

Database designs should be based on the *similarities* between different types of objects. This will make it easier to transfer designs to more complex databases if necessary.

Where possible, design the database so that field names are akin to the most 'general' concepts possible. A very good example of a generalised data schema is the Dublin Core element set (see Section 4.3), which facilitates interoperability between variant systems.

Simplicity

Database design, and all interfaces to the database structure, should be kept as simple as possible. This will aid both data management tasks and the creation of user-friendly interfaces.

Making efficient use of database technology can be demanding. It is necessary to plan for: initial needs analysis, database design, installation, training and support.

Section 6: Resource Delivery and User Issues

SECTION 6.1 RESOURCE DELIVERY ISSUES: AN OVERVIEW

There are two dimensions to ensuring that the resources that have been created are actually used in the manner in which the creator intended:

- Physically delivering the resource
- Mobilising and supporting user's interaction with the resource

1 Physically delivering the resource

This is the final element in a decision chain which would hopefully have commenced in the stages of planning to create a resource. There are two elements to the physical delivery of the resource:

- Delivery mechanism
- Interface design

Delivery mechanism

The delivery mechanism could be CD ROM or via the Internet, for example. Network delivery, via an Intranet or the Internet, certainly seems to be the preferred norm nowadays, with its advantage of access and ease of editing, but serious considerations are involved whichever method is chosen. Questions to ask of access include:

- Are you planning to restrict the resource to particular classes of user (e.g. higher education, or non-profit organisations)?
- Do you want people to register with you before gaining access to it?
- How are you planning to protect the security of your resource?
- Do you have in mind a series of things that users are allowed to do with your material; for example, use it for non-profit making purposes in research and teaching perhaps?
- Do you have in mind a series of things that you explicitly don't want them to do; for example, a student may think it perfectly permissible to download an image from your website and put it up on their Internet home page, if you don't state otherwise!

You need to be quite clear about these matters and ideally have a statement of permitted uses accompanying the delivered resource.

Interface design

The resource interface is the screen design and the tools through which users will search and work with the material. This is a complex area which will require a great deal of careful research and planning, and also require feedback from a wide variety of users (preferably of varying levels of computer literacy). The interface should be tested for its ease of use and also whether searching and browsing brings satisfactory results.

2 Mobilising and supporting users' interactions with the resource

This is a demanding job, particularly if your data are extensive or specialised. It could involve a variety of roles: from trouble shooting with users who are having problems accessing or searching your data, to more structured activities, such as providing specific training or workshops in how your data can be used and applied within different teaching and research scenarios.

Some of the more structured mobilisation activities may also be too resource-intensive for a given institution to undertake in isolation. You may again want to consider working with a data archive or other higher education service, who have been funded to provide support in the management and use of digital resources.

All these issues will be expanded upon in this chapter as follows:

- Section 6.2: interface issues
- Section 6.3: access issues
- Section 6.4: standards for sharing and exchanging networked data
- Section 6.5: user support issues

Out-sourcing delivery

In some cases it may be more appropriate to use a third party to deal with on-line delivery and archiving. For example, VADS provides delivery and preservation services for visual arts resources of research, teaching and learning interest. (For more information about archiving services, see Section 9.2.)

SECTION 6.2 USER INTERFACE AND RETRIEVAL ISSUES

Searching and retrieval methods

One very basic feature of user interaction with electronic data is the methods through which they are encouraged to query and work with a resource's content.

Anticipating user behaviour is not always easy. Sometimes the person with the most intimate knowledge of how the resource has been constructed and what it contains is not the best person to specify how the user will access it. This is because it is often hard to take a step backwards and look at the resource with 'fresh eyes', as if you are coming to it for the first time.

It might be quite obvious to the resource creator how to make the best of searching for and retrieving the contents of the resource, but it is not always the case for a user who may have a limited idea of the kind of information that the resource contains. This is why it is essential to get *feedback* from a variety of potential users throughout the process of constructing the user interface layer.

Many users are well versed in certain kinds of expected interactions with digital resources, particularly in an electronic environment. For example one typical feature of many resources presented via the world wide web is the simple box on screen where you enter a term to search as below:

Search for: [   ]   GO !

Figure 4: Typical WWW search box

This is a fairly basic function and certainly not a difficult concept for a user to handle. However, entering such a term can be like casting thoughts into the wind unless proper thought has been given to the issue of effective data retrieval.

For example it may be the case that a user is searching for Boticelli's *The Primavera*. However it so happens that this particular resource is an Italian website. Although there is much information in English on the site, the individual works of art have been catalogued using their Italian names. In this case, *Il Primavera* is referred to throughout the resource.

When the search button is hit the *search engine* will then use the information entered by the user to construct a query to all the data held on the system. This particular system requires the user to enter the *exact* text or the relevant work of art will not be found. So after entering *The Primavera* the user is returned zero hits and assumes the resource does not contain what the item in question.

A better way of setting up a search engine, therefore, would have been to allow the information that the user has entered to be matched with the contents of the resource in a more flexible manner. A free text search, for example, is something which allows the terms given to be searched across all the contents in the resource.

There are many similar considerations to bear in mind when designing a user access layer, and fortunately most experienced software designers are very aware of these issues and will have established the basic principles of coding to allow flexible and viable searching.

The categories of information that you have associated with the resource will also directly effect how the user accesses it. These are described in Section 4 in more detail.

Querying electronic data is not by any means a simple process; however, the following is a brief guide to the most common searching methods. It is best to employ them as alternative strategies within resources rather than exclusive ones.

1 Browsing

This is where you follow a 'tree' like structure that eventually leads you to the resource you want. At each level, you are presented with a series of options, from which you choose to 'go on'. Thus the 'search-trail' may be Visual Arts – Painting – Modernist – French – Delaunay – Robert. This is an extremely user-friendly method, but can be time-consuming, less direct and inflexible in search results. Many Internet 'libraries' and subject guides, such as YAHOO, employ these.

Particular to image resources, however, is 'thumbnail' browsing. This presents a 'gallery' of small, low resolution, images through which to glance. This is a particularly useful tool if you are merely concerned with sourcing visual material, or already have in mind the image you want, but not necessarily any contextual information.

2 Free text searching
Most Internet search engines and database query languages will offer this facility. Literally the search will interrogate every part of the data for the textual information entered. This will usually produce a large number of successful search-results, but not necessarily a high percentage of contextually accurate ones. Thus further refinement of the search will usually be necessary.

3 Boolean searching
This is a method of refining search criteria. The principal Boolean operators are the logic terms 'AND', 'NOT' and 'OR'. They may be used singularly or in combination to produce subtly differing search results. These simply do as they suggest:

AND narrows a search, by combining two or more terms. Thus 'Sonia AND Robert AND Delaunay, ensures 'hits' which only include all these words appearing in a record, to the exclusion of citations of the artists individually.

OR widens a search and will both combine two or more search terms and also recall where they appear individually. Thus 'Sonia OR Robert AND Delaunay' will return instances where both artists are mentioned in a text and also where one is mentioned but not the other.

NOT again narrows a search, but this time by excluding one term from another. Thus 'Sonia NOT Robert' would only retrieve items from the previous search which solely mentioned the female artist.

4 Visual and content-based retrieval for images
A further set of techniques for searching are those which attempt to use the visual evidence within images to aid retrieval. Using image appearance rather than textual descriptors as a basis for searching is often known as content-based retrieval. Some of these techniques may have specific relevance for art images. An example of an art image retrieval tool is MORELLI, developed by Professor William Vaughan of Birkbeck College. This enables rapid searching of picture archives to locate images which bear a visual resemblance to a chosen image. Commercially available tools are also developing rapidly; perhaps the best known of these is QBIC by IBM (http://wwwqbic.almaden.ibm.com/~qbic/). For a more comprehensive description of these techniques and applications, see the description of research activities in this area at the Institute for Image Data Research at the University of Northumbria (http://www.unn.ac.uk/iidr/CBIR/cbir.html). The IIDR site also includes a useful page of relevant links for this area: http://www.unn.ac.uk/iidr/links.html.

User interface design
What follows is a set of of good practice criteria for the creation of user interfaces, especially for resources delivered via the Internet.

- The use of metaphors – to convey concepts and features. It is a useful method by which to increase the friendliness of a site
- See and point – for the user to interact directly with the screen, by selecting items and performing activities with, for example, a mouse

- Consistency – allows users to transfer knowledge and skills already gained. An example of this is the use of standard link colours. Blue indicates that the user has not yet accessed a link to a new page, and red/purple indicate links to previously seen pages
- Perceived stability – the interface needs to be understandable, predictable and familiar. Do not assign new behaviour to existing features/objects – this adds confusion
- Aesthetic integrity – the information should be well organised and display graphics should be kept simple (keep icons to a minimum, no frames). The use of frames is very confusing as this can break the fundamental user model of the WWW page. It also leads to technical problems such as an inability to bookmark the current page, URLs stop working and printouts become difficult
- Graphic design – leave out insignificant detail; the screen should look clean and free from clutter. The design should be attractive and look good on different bit-depth screens. Sites should try to be non-intrusive by avoiding visual and auditory gimmicks. A page should try to avoid including elements that are constantly moving. Graphics should complement the subject matter – not detract from it.
- Graphics/images – these should be optimised where possible. Large file sizes have a significant importance on accessibility, as they take longer to download
- Quality of information – users are concerned about quality of information and the customer service you can provide. Outdated information should be removed. Maintenance of WWW pages is required to ensure that this is achieved
- Pages – link to home page, navigation, and short pages. Pages should indicate which site they belong to, as lots of users access the pages without coming through the home page. A map should be provided, so that users know where they are and which pages they can/cannot access. Ensure that if the user is accessing the site from a bookmark, all registration procedures (if any) are still operational

Interface design is a dedicated area. Should you not feel confident with it, think about out-sourcing, gaining consultancy or researching further.

SECTION 6.3 CONTROLLING ACCESS

It is necessary to control access to uphold licence agreements and prevent unauthorised use and possible mis-use of data. This is also relevant to copyright and rights management issues. For example, a resource that has been cleared for public dissemination via the Internet would not require special access controls, whilst one which has only been cleared with a specific group of users in mind may need to provide controls to fulfil the licence agreement. (See Section 2 for further details about rights management and licensing issues.)

It is also important to bear in mind that given the current free access culture of the Internet, users often expect to be able to reach information freely and may resent the need to register for resources. Therefore, access control procedures should be as simple for users to interact with as possible. Complicated procedures can deter use.

User registration and authentication

Access to networked resources can be controlled through user registration and authentication. This is aided by security and data protection methods.

Registration

User registration not only controls access to who may view or use a resource, but also permits the formalising of usage agreements and the monitoring of usage.

Formalising usage agreements

The registration process can ensure that the user is aware of, has read the license registration and copyright documents, and agreed to them. By agreeing with these documents the user is then legally bound by them. If there is no registration process there is the likelihood of the user by-passing these documents. Usage agreements should also contain user recognition of and compliance with security procedures.

Monitoring usage

Registration allows statistical analysis of the site to be obtained. This can include analysis by resource-user and by resource-content. For example, what sector of a user community is accessing and using the site? What are their particular areas of interest in the resource? Such information can be used in targeting strategies and to help determine future development of the resource.

Following a registration process, steps will need to be taken to ensure only registered users access the resource. This process requires authentication methods.

Authentication

For networked resources, user authentication can be defined as the process by which a server can restrict access to certain users or subscribers to a service. On the Internet, the home page of a site may be accessible by all users, but the site will often have a secure area only accessible by registered users.

There are currently three methods available for authentication and access control:

- Basic authentication
- IP Filtering
- Basic authentication and IP Filtering combined

1 Basic authentication

This is a relatively simple procedure and involves a user having a username and a password. When the user requests access to a resource or site, the server sends an 'authentication required' message in a dialogue box. The user can then enter their username and password and re-submit the request.

If the username and password combination match a pair kept in the account file, access to the secure area is granted. If not, access is denied.

This method is used when people who are allowed access to the resources are widely dispersed, or the server-administrator needs to control access on an individual basis.

Advantages

- Standardised 'login' procedure for user
- No computer expertise required by user
- Server administrator maintains full control over access rights

Disadvantages

• low level of security

Passwords are easily disclosed to third parties, either knowingly or unknowingly. User-chosen passwords are often guessable and 'given' ones can be difficult to remember and are thus written down and susceptible to loss or theft. Responsibility for password security should be with the user and declared as such in the usage agreement.

Automatic password transmission can also be tracked and decoded in a networked environment. This could allow unauthorised entry under a stolen account. Encrypting basic authentication data will greatly reduce this risk.

This basic method is often inadequate in preventing unauthorised access when used as the only means of authentication.

2 IP Filtering

With IP Filtering, the server checks (pattern matches) the IP address of the client and uses that for authorisation.

Advantages

• More secure than basic authentication
• Restricts users to 'login' from a single (or restricted range of) workstation(s), e.g. from within a particular institution or site

Disadvantages

• May be much harder to manage for the system administrator
• User inconvenience because of limitations in where they can log-on from, for example when working from home
• Possible, though very difficult, for unauthorised users to 'spoof' IP addresses and fool filtering mechanisms.

3 Basic authentication and IP Filtering combined

Advantages

• Double layered authentication (as above)

Disadvantages

• Password insecurity (as above)
• User can only login from one (or a restricted range of) computer(s) (as above)
• Still not 100% secure – no networked resource is impregnable from attack by hackers or determined unregistered users

This last point should not induce panic. Firstly, it is highly unlikely that your resource would be the target of such behaviour. Secondly, if it has been created with the best practices laid out herein, then the following inherent security measures will be 'built in':

- Only 'access' level data would be available to unauthorised users
- Data would be regularly backed-up and hence retrievable, if corrupted
- If the unthinkable occurred and any part of the access data was permanently corrupted, the archival record would be intact to remedy the situation

Higher education registration initiatives

With authentication, the one big problem for users is having to remember too many passwords. As a response to this situation, the Joint Information Systems Committee (JISC) of the Higher Education Funding Council are funding initiatives in this area such as the latest release of ATHENS (http://www.athens.ac.uk/).

The ATHENS service will provide a 'single sign-on' to multiple resources and fully distributed management of user accounts.

A note on data protection

If a digital image archive wishes to register and authenticate their users, then it will no doubt create a database (in the loosest term) of personal information. This has implications for the archive, as all data that are processed automatically have to be registered with the Data Protection Registrar, according to the 1984 Data Protection Act.

The Data Protection Act imposes obligation on data users to:

- Be open about their use of data (through registration)
- To maintain good practice in relation to personal data they hold(2).
- Data users are required to register certain information:
    The personal data they hold
    The purposes that they use it for
    The sources from which they may obtain data
    Those to whom they may disclose the data
    The countries or territories outside the UK to which they may transfer data

Personal data is defined by the 1984 Act as data which relate to a living individual, who can be identified from that information alone, or through other information held by the data user.

It is an offence to hold personal data without being registered. The law applies to data that are processed automatically, but not data that are paper based. It also only applies to personal data about living individuals.

Security and protection of image data

Further protection can be offered to digital images through watermarking practices. This adds an extra security dimension to the images and makes them traceable to the resource they came from and/or the copyright owner.

Digital watermarking

Intellectual property right (IPR) owners of images are often reluctant to make their material available within a networked environment because of the ease of electronic copying and re-transmission. A possible solution to this problem is digital watermarking.

Digital watermarks can contain information to define: the source; the author; the creator; the owner; the distributor and the authorised consumer of the digital image, such as:

- A copyright notice
- A unique serial number
- A creator
- A distributor identifier
- A transaction identifier

One crucial element is required in a watermark – its admissibility in a court of law, as evidence of infringement of copyright. A digital watermark must not be open to interpretation or confusion for it to be legally valid. Thus a digital watermark must be embedded within a digital image such that it can be detected later without any errors.

There are two types of digital watermark available: visible and invisible.

Visible digital watermarking

Visible watermarks can simply be a case of putting a logo on a corner of the image, such that the origin of that image is known. Alternatively, the logo can obscure the majority or an essential part of the image to ensure the on-line image is of no commercial use. Any removal or tampering with the logo would break the copyright agreement.

Another way is to write the copyright notice and other information into an extra couple of lines within the image file. The extra lines can be removed from the image, without detriment to the image quality and content, but this again would break the copyright agreement of the image.

Advantages

- Relatively simple procedure

Disadvantages

- Easily removed
- Can infringe on image content

Invisible digital watermarking

Invisible digital watermarks involve the embedding of information into the digital image file such that it is unviewable by the human eye.

To be effective in the protection of the ownership of intellectual property, an invisibly watermarked image should satisfy several criteria:

- The watermark must be difficult or impossible to remove, at least without visibly degrading the original image
- The watermark must survive image modifications that are typical image-processing applications (e.g. scaling, colour correction, dithering, cropping and image compression and printing)
- An invisible watermark should be imperceptible so as not to affect the experience of viewing the image

- For some invisible watermarking applications, watermarks should be readily detectable by the proper authorities, even if imperceptible to the average observer. Such decodability without requiring the original, un-watermarked image would be necessary for efficient recovery of property and subsequent prosecution
  Current commercial systems available for watermarking digital images include:
- Digimarc Corporation have software which works with Adobe PhotoShop, Corel Draw and Corel PHOTO-PAINT.
  (http://www.digimarc.com/applications/copyright/copyright_in.html)
- Suresign by Signum Technologies Ltd, has plug-ins for both readers and detectors for Adobe PhotoShop.
  (http://www.signumtech.com/suresign/index.html)

Advantages

- Higher level of security
- No infringement on image quality

Disadvantages

- Requires specialised software
- Does not act as a visible deterrent within the image

The application of digital watermarking and other access controls to resources is a question of risk assessment and the requirements of copyright holders.

SECTION 6.4 STANDARDS FOR DATA INTERCHANGE

So far, this section has dealt with the *data documentation and metadata* which allows resources to be searched for and retrieved more efficiently via networks. The aim here is to introduce and explicate the notion of *cross resource searching*.

Here is an example: A researcher is sourcing material for a thesis on 'war, art and western civilisation'. In the current situation, they would perhaps do an Internet search via a particular catalogue, initially entering the search term 'war and art'. The resulting series of 'hits' produces an enormous variety of items. From these, access is gained to a number of records from the Imperial War Museum Art Collection database, which VADS is making available via the Internet. The researcher is pleased with the results of this search.

However as the research topic is quite broad, other on-line archives are required. Another archive is accessed, which holds abstracts of articles on art. The researcher comes back with a series of 'hits' of bibliographic citations from journals on the subject.

The researcher then enters another two museum and gallery sites and a further on-line archive, searches on 'war and art', and comes back with a number of results (not all of which are relevant), covering objects in museums and galleries. All this has taken quite some time. Overall, interacting with all these different systems has been a relatively long and frustrating process and s/he is beginning to question whether searching on the Internet is the best method of carrying out this research!

However, imagine the same scenario again: This time, all the different on-line archives searched are 'linked up' or 'interoperable'. The user would therefore be able to enter a 'search gateway', enter a search term and get back results from all the various archives simultaneously. The researcher would obviously need to consider how broad or narrow the search should be so as not to get results which are too broad. However, in this one search a series of results have been obtained which will also give a good indication of the contents of each archive, and offers the option to go to a particular archive for more in-depth searching later.

This ideal scenario does put the onus on *data creators* to make it feasible for information to be exchanged between different on-line catalogues, as Section 4 advises. Systems that allow such interchanges of data do so through the application of data-exchange 'protocols'. A commonly used protocol in the libraries, museums and archival community is Z39.50.

Z39.50

Z39.50 is a data protocol that allows disparate databases to *interoperate* with one another. A 'query' is entered on one terminal and sent to a Z39.50 enabled 'client' server. This 'intermediary' server establishes the form of Z39.50 the query is produced in and then opens up a connection to the 'target' database. The 'target' dataset is then checked for its Z39.50 capabilities, thus enabling the query to be matched in a viable manner to the data on the 'target' system. This is followed by a Z39.50 'transacted' query result being returned to the terminal that requested the information. For the user this process appears as 'seamless' and the need to enter a different search interface or contact a completely new system is negated.

An example of a Z39.50 enabled system is the Arts and Humanities Data Service (AHDS) Internet Gateway, which can interrogate across all AHDS Service Providers' catalogues. http://ahds.ac.uk

It is worth acknowledging that these interchange protocols may not be something that data creators can implement on an individual basis, as it is dependent upon their delivery systems. However, it is certainly important to be aware of them and what potential there is. This potential can be realised through depositing completed resources with a third-party Z39.50 enabled system, such as VADS/AHDS.

SECTION 6.5 USER SUPPORT ISSUES

As has been suggested, it is easy to make assumptions about *who* your user base for a digital resource may be and *what* they will attempt to do with it. However, it is evident that producing the digital resource and successfully delivering it to the user is only the beginning of the story. There will be continuing work to be done in educating users in the best ways to take advantages of the new resources currently on offer.

This is exacerbated by the fact that at present there are very varying levels of computer literacy in the visual arts community. Some are accustomed to using digital resources delivered via the Internet, internal networks or CD ROMs, for example, as a means of research and study as well as relying on paper-based materials. To others, however, these types of resource simply do not have a place in their patterns of research, teaching or learning. They may also feel that it is not worth the time and effort to learn the new skills that are needed to engage with digital resources. While the presence of the Internet and networked resources is difficult for anyone to ignore, many potential users argue that what is being offered is not of a sufficiently high quality and that they do not have the necessary computer equipment to access what is on offer. This is certainly borne out by a survey of engagement with digital resources undertaken by VADS in November 1997, a chart from which is reproduced below. (http://vads.ahds.ac.uk/survey1.html).

A snapshot of users' requirements when engaging with the digital resource and the extent to which these needs are being answered within higher education contexts is provided in the following report, which examines the broader context of the arts and humanities. This also contains details of a specific workshop held by VADS to subject the findings of our survey to further examination (*Scholars' Information Requirements in a Digital Age*). http://ahds.ac.uk/public/uneeds/un0.html

However despite the patchiness of current ability and willingness to engage with the digital, this situation is clearly changing rapidly, with levels of computer literacy and of acceptance of the potential of new resources developing exponentially. While it is still the case that the number and nature of new digital resources available is outpacing peoples' ability to engage with them, there are strategies which, if implemented, will increase the level of user satisfaction

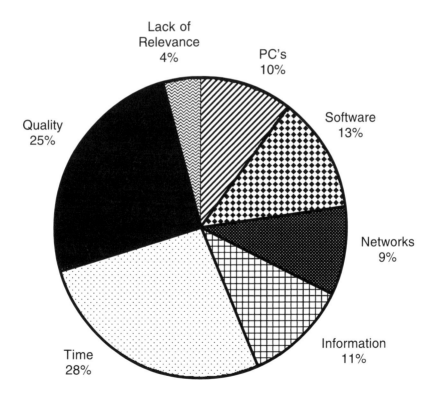

Figure 5: Problems when using electronic resources

with the digital resource and so in turn justify the investments that are currently being made. A few of these strategies are outlined below.

Dealing with user queries

The extent and nature of questions from users you will experience once you have delivered a new digital resource will obviously depend on the size of your intended audience and the complexity of what you have created. It is likely that a specific teaching resource, for example, delivered to students in a controlled manner will have a fairly defined, and also often repeated, set of questions associated with its use. However you may have produced something, for example a detailed archival record of contemporary installation and sculpture, using a multimedia environment delivered via the Internet to a wide audience, which could attract a bewildering array of questions and problems. Failure to answer these in what the user feels is an adequate time-span can cause immense frustration. It is also reported in common 'techno-lore', in which there is probably more than a grain of truth, that the 'average user will only attempt to get to a piece of information three times (or three mouse clicks), before abandoning the search and using another website or other resource. From this perspective it is crucial that the user has as easy and productive an encounter with the data as can be feasibly provided. Questions of usability and accessibility also of course relate to the quality of the data interface, see Section 6.2.

The types of user queries concerning the use of digital data fall into the following two general categories:

*   Technical – *'I cannot access your site, my password doesn't work'* (if the site is protected) *'I have forgotten my password'*. *'The images look funny on my web browser, what shall I do?' 'Every time I access your site my computer crashes' etc.*
*   Content – queries about what your resource contains, from the very specific to the bewilderingly vague – *'I see you have a sculpture in here which looks very similar to a picture I saw in a magazine last week, is it likely to be by the same person?'* to, *'Do you have an image of Anthony Gormley's Angel of the North while still under construction taken at sunset?'*

Therefore to answer the range of questions likely to be posed by users, you will probably need to have both technical support and subject-based knowledge on hand to keep users engaged, interested in, and positive about what you are providing. These demands will obviously intensify in situations where a resource is being charged for in some respect, in which case the relationship between the data provider and user becomes more akin to that of the product and its market place.

In this kind of scenario, you may want to attempt to control the process of user enquiry. This is difficult, but there are mechanisms that may help. For example publicising a specific help desk service with well advertised hours of operation, response time and type of assistance available will help to temper user expectations of the help you can provide.

It is also worth making the point that if you are envisaging developing a broad base of access for your resource via an on-line environment and you do not have the support locally for this development you may want to outsource this side of your resource delivery. This is one of the services provided by the Visual Arts Data Service.

It is also the case that the more detailed level of documentation you have about how your system works, what it contains and how it may be accessed, the more sustainable and viable your resource will be. This documentation will enable your current users as well as future generations to make sense not only of what is immediately apparent to them, but also the intentionality or reasoning behind what has been created.

Raising awareness

Once your investment in a digital resource has been made, it is likely that you will want to publicise it widely to its intended audience(s) and to make sure that it is appreciated and used as you intended. As commented in the introduction to this section, there are clearly barriers which may prevent users from appreciating and even gaining access to what has been created. However in the last two years this situation has developed considerably, with digital materials and the Internet becoming part of the everyday culture and fabric of our society. This means some of the barriers to take up will remove themselves naturally. In the interim phase, however, often more positive and proactive measures need to be taken to introduce the digital into traditional teaching, research and learning environments. Also on a more simple level, because of the proliferation of electronic information of a variable quality, it becomes ever more important to ensure that awareness is sufficient to bring interested parties to a given resource.

You may also want to raise awareness of your resource by lodging it in a data archive where it will join a critical mass of relevant material; for example the extensive holdings of the Arts and Humanities Data Service (http://ahds.ac.uk). Furthermore it may also prove appropriate to consider sharing the costs of awareness raising materials and events with other organisations who also have a stake or interest in what you have achieved.

What follows are some practical suggestions for methods of awareness raising:

Setting up an electronic mailing list

An electronic mailing list operates via e-mail, where messages can be sent to or from a list which will then reach a series of subscribed members who are interested in receiving information or discussing the lists subject e.g. 'contemporary art'. You can set up a list so that it is open, i.e. anyone can join and send information, or closed, where only users you have approved and added can send and receive messages from the list. It is also the case that a list community tends to set itself up, where messages you send will be posted on to other relevant lists, and you yourself can join other lists and publicise your activities that way. In this manner a broad audience can be reached with minimal effort and investment of time. An example of this comprehensive list service is that provided by JISCmail, which holds 2,388 discussion lists and has 164,805 members world-wide. JISCmail is free to the UK higher education community. It is also worth noting that members of organisations or private individuals outside the UK higher education community are free to join lists, and furthermore JISCmail also offers a fee-paying list service for those who want to set up new lists outside this community. For instructions about how to set up or join a list, see the JISCmail Website (http://www.jiscmail.ac.uk/).

Contact database

If resources permit, it is recommended that you set up a database with names and addresses of those who have an interest in accessing or developing the use of your resource. Once this has been established, it can act as the basis of a mailing list for newsletters, announcements and other publicity materials.

Networking

It is an obvious point, but if you attend conferences, events etc. relevant to your subject area, awareness will grow of what you have achieved, usage will develop and increase, and you will also have the opportunity to define your own goals in the light of others experience and achievements. In the Visual Arts community there are many relevant annual events. For example, the following organisations all hold annual conferences, all of which are concerned wholly or partially with issues surrounding the generation and use of digital resources:

- CADE (Computers in Art and Design Education)
  This is a bi-annual conference; the 1999 conference was held at the University of Teeside http://www.tees.ac.uk/cade99. The next conference will be hosted by Glasgow School of Art in 2001.
- CHArt (Computers and the History of Art)
  Chart holds an annual conference. A general website about Chart giving details of conferences and membership is at (http://www.hart.bbk.ac.uk/chart/)
- MDA (Museum Documentation Association)
  For details about the MDA and its annual conferences, see (http://w.mda.org.uk/)
- ARLIS (Art Libraries Association)
  Events are listed at (http://arlis.nal.vam.ac.uk)
- DRH (Digital Resources in the Humanities)
  An annual conference is held at various venues which brings together those interested in the creation and use of digital resources in the arts and humanities. The conference website is at (http://w.drh.org.uk/).

Training and workshops

It may be appropriate for you to host specific training events where users come and receive instruction from you, ideally in a hands-on environment, on how to best make use of your resource. If your audience does have clear and contained boundaries, then such a mechanism, though time-consuming to set up can be an effective method of reaching multiple users, and therefore circumventing repetitive user enquiries.

If you do have a very broad set of users in mind who would be impossible to reach through one or even a series of events, you may want to consider joining forces with other organisations. For example the Visual Arts Data Service currently runs training and dissemination events in conjunction with other organisations and projects involved in this area, in particular TASI. While training has focused on developing general skills, for example, raising awareness of copyright issues, it will become increasingly resource-based, and therefore highly relevant to the demands of training related to a particular resource. In particular, workshops will be organised to introduce users to and develop the use of the on-line collections VADS is delivering.

Section 7: Storage and Preservation

SECTION 7.1 STORAGE

Introduction

This section looks at storage and digital preservation issues. Firstly, storage issues and storage media, necessary for holding and backing up 'work in progress' and 'local archiving' are discussed. This is followed by an introduction to digital preservation as a concept, preservation strategies, the global preservation arena and the benefits of depositing with a *third party digital archive*.

Introducing storage issues

Storage is a concern at all phases of the digitisation chain, from capture, through to archiving. Storage can be thought of in terms of 'portable' and 'non-portable' media.

Portable media

Portable media each have a limited capacity per unit; storage capacity is therefore extendable only by increasing the number of units. The following table indicates types of portable media currently available and their capacities.

Portable media are susceptible to technological change and their degree of platform compatibility and driver requirements are variable.

Media	Typical Unit Capacity up to:
Floppy disks	1.4MB
ZIP disks	100MB
JAZ disks	2GB
DAT	4GB
CD-ROM	650MB
DVD	17GB
DVT	40GB

Table 4: A comparison of types of portable media and their capacities

Non-portable media

These media generally provide much higher storage capacities and transfer rates, which vary by make and model. Non-portable media include:

- Hard drives (PC disks)
- Network drives (server disks)
- Data warehousing

Capacities can be increased by replacing or adding drives, dependent on the overall system configuration.

Storage needs

File storage space is required for:

- Work in progress
- Backing-up
- Local archiving
- Third party archiving

Work in progress

Depending on the resource creation 'set-up', work in progress, will either be stored on a hard-disk local to a PC, or on a network server-disk area. It could also be a combination of the two. The specification for each will depend upon the projected storage needs of the resource creation exercise, that is the total file sizes to be produced.

Backing-up

This means creating a *safe copy* of work in progress. This should occur at various stages of resource creation, to ensure work is saved and available to be worked on, should the 'primary' storage facility fail or be inaccessible. Backing-up may be to a portable media and/or network disk space.

Local archiving

Following the completion of resource creation, or each of its phases, it is good practice to create an 'archive' copy. This copy could be on either portable or non-portable media and should be subject to 'preservation strategies' to ensure the longevity of the resource and/or its component parts (see Section 7.3).

Third party archiving

Third party archiving should ensure the longevity of a resource, through the guarantee of *digital data stability* and preservation strategies to ensure a resource's long-term *accessibility*. Although transfer to third party archives, may require the use of portable media, once delivered, resources are likely to reside in 'data warehousing' facilities and/or on-line delivery systems. A fuller exposition of the benefits of third-party archiving is given in Section 7.4.

Storage requirements through resource creation phases

Storage requirements are considered for:

- Primary acquisition and 'master/archival' files
- Surrogate/delivery files

1 Primary acquisition and 'master/archival' files

Primary acquisition and 'master/archival' files, especially those of images, will have the largest storage requirements. In terms of digital images this can be over 10 times more than for surrogate 'electronic delivery' type images.

Storage requirements at this stage of the creation process are thus likely to be *very high*, dependent on the number of images involved and their accompanying metadata. This is both in terms of hard-disk/server space for 'work in progress' and 'back-up'/'local archive' media, whether on local, networked or portable media.

If maintaining 'local archive' copies of 'primary acquisition' or 'master/archival files' on portable media, it is essential to store them under the right conditions, have them properly identified and a strategy in place for their long-term survival (see Section 7.3 for further discussion of preservation strategies).

2 Surrogate/delivery files

Storage requirements for these types of file are likely to be far less in terms of capacities than for the above. Again, if locally archiving such data it is important to have a proper preservation strategy in place (see section 7.3).

Storage media and archiving

None of the media mentioned above has yet been around long enough to be fully proven as a long-term viable storage medium. For this reason the following are good practices to observe when selecting storage media for *archiving locally*:

- Write 'archive' data to at least two different types of media
- Hold archive copies in variant locations
- Subject the media to traditional collections management routines:
    Store under correct environmental conditions
    Observe handling recommendations of the media

To ensure the best possible long-term survival of digital resources, it is advisable to have a preservation strategy in place and to consider archiving with a third-party specialist organisation. (Sections 7.3 and 7.4 discuss this further.)

SECTION 7.2 INTRODUCING DIGITAL PRESERVATION

Introduction

Digital preservation should be an integral consideration when creating a digital resource for the visual arts. Considering preservation/archiving needs and having a digital preservation strategy on board, from the planning stage of a resource, will ensure the longevity and accessibility of the data produced and maximise the investment made in data creation.

Digital preservation is a relatively new concept, and hence is currently a specialised area, synonymous with 'third party archiving', although the strategies developing (see Section 7.3) can be utilised at a 'local' level.

This section acts as an introduction to digital preservation and the issues of concern.

Defining digital preservation

Beagrie and Greenstein (1998) describe digital preservation as *'the preservation of digital materials and the preservation of paper based materials and other artifacts through their digitisation'*. (Beagrie and Greenstein, 1998. *A Strategic Policy Framework for Creating and Preserving Digital Collections* [online] London: Kings College, London. Available from: http://ahds.ac.uk/manage/framework.htm)

Margaret Hedstrom describes digital preservation as *'retaining the ability to display, retrieve, manipulate and use the digital information in the face of constantly changing technology'*. (The Task Force for the Archiving of Digital Information 1996. *Preserving Digital Information* [online] California Commission for the Preservation of Access, and The Research Libraries Group. Available from: http://www.rlg.org/ArchTF/)

These definitions of digital preservation address two important concepts.

- Digitisation can be utilised for preserving both digital *and* analogue materials.
- Digital preservation provides the ability to ensure the long-term access and use of digital materials.

The concept of digital preservation that this section specifically addresses is the preservation of digital, rather than analogue, materials.

Aims of digital archiving

These are summarised by Lievesley, D. 1995. Strategies for Managing Electronic Resource. *Long Term Preservation of Electronic Materials* [online], JISC, and The British Library as:

- Preserving the physical reliability of data
- Ensuring the continued usability of the data
- Integrating data into information and dissemination systems
- Securing data from unauthorised access

Digital preservation is thus not only about securing the long-term stability and single-use of data: archiving can permit increased access to and use of resources. In terms of specialised third-party archiving this can mean that added value is placed on a resource, by integrating it into a robust and dedicated information and dissemination system of like material.

SECTION 7.3 INTRODUCING DIGITAL PRESERVATION STRATEGIES

In theory, data that has been encoded into a binary digital form can be preserved in perpetuity, by storing and checking the 'bit-stream' (machine-readable code) of the resource. However, the changing technological environment means there are significant 'access' challenges to preserving data that require extra archival strategies.

Digital preservation strategies include:

* Refreshing
* Migration
* Emulation
* Standardisation

The first three apply to resources *after* they have been created, though they should be planned for, whereas standardisation should be applied as part of the creation process itself, to aid digital preservation.

Refreshing

This relates to preserving media only. Refreshing is simply copying the digital files from one storage device to another of the same type.

This method is viable only when the digital files are in a non-proprietary format and independent of hardware and software. If the files are in a proprietary format, problems may arise when refreshing the media, as changes to the specifications of the file format may have been implemented by the format owner. In such cases, difficulty may be experienced, when accessing the files. (Hardware and software will still be required to read non-proprietary formats.)

Because of problems with 'backward compatibility' and 'interoperability', refreshing is not viewed as an effective solution to long-term digital preservation.

Migration

This is the transferral of data to a different type of media and format, as necessary. The purpose of migration is to preserve the integrity of digital objects and to retain the ability to retrieve, display and otherwise use them in the face of constantly changing technology (The Task Force on Archiving of Digital Information, 1996).

Records should be migrated to new media and/or formats before the current ones deteriorate or become obsolete. Both periodic inspections of storage media to identify any deterioration and continuing review of the evolution of the technology for signs of obsolescence are needed to determine when to migrate records (International Council of Archives, 1996).

Emulation

This is a strategy where the technology has grown from the computer gaming arena. Rather than attempting to migrate files continually into new versions of software which is compatible with new hardware functionalities, emulation instead involves constructing software that will run 'defunct' files on current or variant systems 'as if' they were running on the system they were originally designed for.

Standardisation

This is a strategy which alleviates hardware/software differences, at their root: resource creation. The adoption of standard formats for digital content and accompanying metadata ensures that resources will have greater interoperability and compatibility between variant systems and increased longevity.

Preservation issues and checklist

Whichever preservation strategy is employed to ensure the longevity of a digital resource, the main objective will usually be to maintain its *intellectual integrity*.

Kenney and Chapman state this as: *'the long-term value of digital collections should be defined by their intellectual content, not limited by technical decisions made at any point along the digitisation chain'* (Kenney, A. R. and Chapman, S. 1996. Digital Imaging for Libraries and Archives, Department of Preservation and Conservation, Cornell University Library).

The following checklist of preservation strategies for resource creation and planning, based on Kenney and Chapman's work, bears this in mind:

- Gain rights clearance to include preservation activities
- Digitise at a level of quality in line with the information content of analogue originals
- Use non-proprietary systems components, standards and open systems architecture
- Use *standard* digital formats and lossless compression techniques where compression is needed
- Use accepted metadata standards and vocabularies
- Make appropriate back-up copies (machine and human-readable if necessary) for 'disaster recovery'
- Maintain correct environmental storage conditions
- Monitor both media and formats, recopying and reformatting data as necessary
- Migrate data and metadata between generations of technology
- Anticipate and plan for technological development
- Deposit significant resources in archival homes such as those offered by VADS

SECTION 7.4 THE GLOBAL DIGITAL PRESERVATION ARENA

With the ever growing volume of 'digital content' being produced, in a rapidly developing technological environment, the need has been recognised in recent years for digital preservation institutions and initiatives to be developed. These seek to research and/or implement systems for the guaranteed long-term stability and accessibility of digital materials. These include:

- CEDARS
- National Preservation Office (NPO)
- Time and Bits: Managing Digital Continuity
- PADI: Preserving Access to Digital Information
- PRESERV (Research Libraries Group)
- AHDS
- VADS

CEDARS
A UK HE funded project which aims to address the strategic, methodological and practical issues and will provide guidance for libraries in best practice for digital preservation.
http://www.leeds.ac.uk/cedars/

National Preservation Office
The NPO is there to ensure the preservation and continued access to library and archive material. They are doing a lot of research into the preservation of digital materials, all of which contribute to the development of preservation.
http://w.bl.uk/services/preservation/

Time and Bits: Managing Digital Continuity
Proceedings of a meeting held in the Getty Centre in February 1998, to discuss the future uses of digital technologies and their impact on the documentation of cultural heritage.
http://www.getty.edu/gci/conservation/13_1/gcinews/GCINews04.html

PADI: Preserving Access to Digital Information
An Australian site which has information about how to preserve digital information, as well as listings of international conferences, case studies and glossaries.
http://w.w.nla.gov.au/dnc/tf2001/padi/

PRESERV
A program run by the Research Libraries Group (http://www.rlg.org/) which runs projects and activities that support local institutions in their efforts to preserve and thereby improve access to endangered research materials.
http://w.rlg.org./preserv/index.html

Arts and Humanities Data Service (AHDS)
A UK higher education, JISC funded service, the AHDS offers digital preservation and archival services through five subject-based 'Service Providers' and a central executive. Service Providers maintain integral Internet accessible archive collections and these are interoperable through a single AHDS Internet gateway, managed by the executive. Research, training and publicity services in digital resource management and digital preservation are also available.
http://ahds.ac.uk

Visual Arts Data Service (VADS)
VADS provides a digital preservation and Internet deliverable archive service to the visual arts community, as well as promoting and publicising standards and good practices in the management of digital resources.
http://vads.ahds.ac.uk

Benefits of third party archiving
Even if archival services are available locally, utilising the services of a professional dedicated preservation and archiving body will enhance a resource's long-term survivability and can also

add extra use-value to the resource. Not only will third party archiving provide an additional secure repository for data, but through integration into a 'recognised' body of material, it can increase access and use of a resource, whilst publicising materials and their creators.

Benefits of depositing with VADS

Preservation of valuable research data
There is nothing to lose and everything to gain by depositing a copy of a resource with VADS. Electronic data is particularly vulnerable to loss, damage or obsolescence.

Dissemination and access
Letting others have access to data is important for two reasons. First, it facilitates communication within the visual arts community, enhancing the reputation of resource creation organisations and leading to the cross-fertilisation of ideas which results in scholarly excellence. Second, sharing data actually helps in its preservation. The more systems a dataset is copied into, the greater the chance of its survival.

Professional cataloguing and application of standards
Resources will be professionally catalogued by VADS in accordance with existing and emerging documentation and technical standards. This will mean that data can be accessed by others in a meaningful and consistent manner which will maximise the value of deposited resources.

Professional recognition
All VADS datasets will undergo a rigorous process of review by subject specialists. This will mean that the VADS holdings will be recognised as a body of material of a high scholarly quality.

Making a contribution
Depositing your data with VADS is a clear investment in the future of the scholarly community in the visual arts. The constraints on resources over the last few years are a clear reality for most scholars. Therefore it is especially important to ensure the longevity of existing resources and to encourage and facilitate their re-use for the visual arts community.

Section 8: Introducing Specialised Digital Formats

8.1 INTRODUCTION

Visual arts resources, by their very nature and the nature of their user-communities, are likely to benefit from a high degree of visual representation, stimulus and interactivity. This is whether they are created as an information resource for researchers or as 'tools' to aid practitioners and educators. This section looks at some of the technologies which can be used to create enhanced applications and/or be applied to high-quality standards compliant resources to develop their usability further.

Due to the development of computers over the past few years in terms of capacity and operating speeds, it is now far easier to create animations, virtual reality landscapes and 3–D designs etc. to aid the creation, presentation and delivery of digital resources to the visual arts community. The range of software is vast, from computer-aided design to multimedia authoring and animation packages.

Alongside such 'stand-alone' software developments, the functionality of web publishing has also increased greatly and the web now supports a high degree of interactivity and visual possibilities, including 3–D 'virtual reality' (VR) and animations.

These advancements in technology allow the creation of a range of interesting and dynamic resources which are stimulating for the visual arts user. Such enhancements can be achieved as a goal from the outset of a project, or at a later stage, due to the flexibility of high-quality standards compliant digital materials.

This section looks at the following methods which can be explored to create and/or enhance digital resources.

- Web authoring and JAVA
- Virtual Reality
- Computer Aided Design (CAD)
- Interactive multimedia
- Animation and moving images

This section does not provide a full exposition of each but instead offers an introduction to the technologies involved and a taster of the possibilities each offers.

8.2 WEB AUTHORING AND JAVA

The explosion of the Internet and World Wide Web (WWW) as a communication media for research communities and the public beyond has made it the prime delivery media for digital resources. Many software applications now offer automatic web-enabling facilities for the resources they create, and there are numerous 'web-editors' and 'web-management' software packages available. These permit users to create and publish web documents as easily as word-processing packages allow print-document creation. However, to gain the best out of such tools it is useful to understand the medium and its organisational and technical infrastructures.

This section introduces web authoring, Hypertext Mark-up Language (HTML), and web programming: JAVA.

HTML – Hypertext Mark-up Language

Creating a web-document is not programming as such but 'encoding' or 'marking-up' the *content* of a document. The content can include text, images and other digital objects. HTML is the set of 'mark-up' codes which are inserted into a file intended for display on a Web browser. The browser is able to interpret the code, thus allowing the content to be displayed for the user.

Individual elements of the content, e.g. a heading or paragraph, is encapsulated within 'code-identifiers' or 'formatting descriptors' that allow the browser to distinguish it from other types of content and thus re-present the material in a standardised manner. Formatting descriptors are called 'tags'.

Generally, HTML tags come in pairs, one to tell the browser where the 'formatting' starts and another where it ends. All end tags include a back-slash before the 'descriptor'.

Tags are distinguished from the text of a document by placing them in triangular brackets, e.g. the tag <HTML> immediately tells the browser it is dealing with a web-readable HTML document and </HTML> would indicate where the web-readable part of the document ends. Thus the first tags that appear in a HTML document will be the HTML tag (this will usually be qualified by the version of HTML the document is coded in).

To view the HTML 'source code' of a web document simply choose 'View...source' from the menu at the top of a web-browser.

In another example, the tag <H1> means highest level heading and any text appearing between that tag and the tag </H1> will be formatted as per a highest level heading, thus distinguishing it from normal paragraph text and other level headings.

More detailed formatting, such as alignment, colour of text, font size, tables etc. can all be defined by various tags or left as per 'browser defaults'.

'Qualification' of tags, e.g. specifying exactly what the background colour of a page is are usually achieved by placing an 'equals' sign in the tag, e.g <background color=red>

There are syntax rules that govern how code can be written, but it can be written in the simplest text tool, such as 'Notepad' and then read as a fully formatted document in a browser. This makes web-authoring 'simple' in terms of the software required.

Three important tags to be aware of are:

- 'head': <HEAD> </HEAD>
- 'body' <BODY> </BODY>
- 'hyperlink' tags <a href> </a>

Head tag <HEAD> </HEAD>

This tag appears at the beginning of the document, usually immediately after the HTML tag. Within it is defined all the formatting elements that pertain to the *document as a whole*, e.g. background colour, title of page, link colours etc. This is read first by the browser and the information within it, such as the title of the page is displayed in browser information areas, such as bookmarks.

Body tag <BODY> </BODY>

This contains all the formatting, that pertains to the main 'body' of the document and defines how the document appears in the scrollable document area of the browser.

Hyperlink tags <a href> </a>

These are the tags that can be used to link elements in web documents, either to other elements within the same document, to other documents within the same site, or to any web document, or part thereof, published anywhere on the web.

These are therefore the tags which turn text into 'hypertext', that is they make web elements 'hot' or 'clickable'. The first <a href> tag needs to include the 'address' or 'url' to go to. For example text encapsulated by <a href="http://vads.ahds.ac.uk"> </a> would link the user to VADS web-site home-page, if 'clicked' on. Hyperlink tags can be attached to images and other objects, as well as text.

HTML standards

The World Wide Web Consortium, (W3C), has a standards committee to define HTML, as well as 'proprietary extenders' of the mark-up language (for example Microsoft and Netscape). Until recently, it was HTML 3.2 which was the official version of this mark-up language. This has now been upgraded to HTML 4.0, which gives the opportunity to develop web pages even further. The W3C web-site carries comprehensive details of all web authoring issues at: http://www.w3.org/

HTML example

A good way to get a grasp on HTML is to view some HTML code. Below is an example of HTML code for the introduction to the VADS case studies page, as first published on our web-site.

The HTML tags are in **bold**. To see what this example of HTML looked like when read by a browser, please see Appendix 3

HTML code for appendix:

<HTML>
<HEAD>
<TITLE>Case Studies**</TITLE>**
<HEAD>

```
<BODY TEXT="#000000" BGCOLOR="#FFFFFF" LINK="#FF0000" VLINK="#8000
40" ALINK="#FF8080">
<P>
<A HREF="index.html"><IMG SRC="/graphics/contents-button-w.gif"BORDER=0
HEIGHT=51WIDTH=51></A>
<A HREF="index.html"><IMG SRC="/graphics/VADS-button-w.gif"BORDER=0
HEIGHT=51WIDTH=251></A>
<A HREF="http://ahds.ac.uk"><IMG SRC+"/graphics/ahds-button-w.gif"BORDER=0
HEIGHT=51WIDTH=70></A>
<BR><BR>
<IMG SRC="/graphics/ahds-rub.gif" HEIGHT=2 WIDTH=437>
</P>
</CENTER>
<CENTER>
<P>
<B>
<FONT SIZE=+3><FONT COLOR="#FF0000">V</FONT>
ADS 
<FONT COLOR="#FF0000">C</FONT>
ase <FONT COLOR="#FF0000">S</FONT>
tudies</FONT>
</B>
</P>
</CENTER>
<CENTER>
<P>An integral part of the work of the Visual Arts Data Service is identifying examples of
current practice from projects involved with the digitisation of visual art material. These case
studies will be a key source of evidence on which to base our guidelines for recommended
practice. It is also apparent that it will only be possible to make practical recommendations to
the community that are based on the experience of recent data creators, calling on what can be
learnt from their achievements and also from the problems they have experienced. </P>
</CENTER>
</BODY>
</HTML>
```

Web authoring issues

There are several different types of Web browser, and when authoring Web pages it is important to remember that people will be viewing the pages in different manners and on different screen settings. It is thus useful to work to the likeliest 'lowest common denominator' of 'target' browser specifications, or to 'flag-up' the best suitable browser/viewing specifications, on the 'home-page'.

Learning web-authoring

There are a number of on-line tutorials for HTML. One of the best introductions to the Internet and HTML is TONIC, which can be found at: http://www.netskills.ac.uk/TONIC/. This is run by Netskills in Newcastle: http://www.netskills.ac.uk/.

Introducing JAVA

Developed by Sun Microsystems, JAVA is a programming language which is *'simple, object-orientated, distributed, interpreted, robust, secure, architecture neutral, portable, high-performance, multi-threaded and dynamic'* JAVA Source Book.

JAVA is a programming language which is platform independent allowing the applications it creates (known as applets) to be run on any machine, be it Macintosh, IBM/PC, UNIX and so on. These applets contain all the information they need to run themselves. However, in order for machines to execute a Java applet they will need an interpreter built into them so that the information can be read, deciphered and displayed in the requested fashion. (Version 3.0 and above web-browsers, are all JAVA enabled.)

The use of an applet allows all machines to read the information and to display it in the requested manner. By enclosing all the information needed for the application within the applet it is much easier to download. One of the most prominent ways in which Java is being used in Web design is to create animated and/or interactive effects.

JAVA in the visual arts

In the visual arts JAVA can be used to create some interesting results, including demonstrating the Golden Section, (http://www.calculator.com/calcs/calc_goldentest.html) and bringing Kandinsky Figurines to life (http://pweb.uunet.de/appel.hh/Java/Figurinen/index-en.html). These examples show how a dynamic interactive environment can be realised with JAVA.

Learning JAVA

Some JAVA elements, e.g. 'roll-overs', are realisable with web-editors without needing to learn specifically how to write JAVA. However, in order to gain the most from JAVA for web-design, it is advisable to learn the language, or 'out-source' the skills. In theory anyone can learn a programming language, but some knowledge of programming, for example C++, will facilitate the learning curve and implementation of JAVA. There are a number of tutorials available over the Internet to learn how to use JAVA, one of the most prominent being The JAVA Tutorial, run by SUN available at: http://java.sun.com:80/docs/books/tutorial/index.html

As the web continues to develop, the degree and quantity of dynamic and interactive resources will undoubtedly increase for the benefits of the visual arts community. Basing the creation of those resources on standards compliant practices suitable for archiving will ensure that enduring benefits can be spread across the community as a whole.

8.3 VIRTUAL REALITY AND VRML

Virtual Reality (VR) is a three-dimensional space in which the user can view, move and rotate around digital objects. VR can be used in a number of scenarios, the most popular vision of which is via a headset where the user feels as though they are physically immersed within a digitally created environment. Other media for viewing VR include on-screen and within hemispherums, which have computer models projected onto them.

VR's most common application within the visual arts is probably in regard to architectural models. These employ CAD packages (see Section 8.4) to allow the user to *envisage and explore* three-dimensional space. This may either be in terms of models of new designs, placed within existing digitised environments, or of reconstructed buildings in past or present settings, for comparison and analysis.

Another common visual arts use for VR is within applied design practice to create three-dimensional models of 'prototypes' to aid design and production assessment.

However, VR is increasingly becoming an option within which to present information-based resources; that is, the use of VR as an *interface* to resources. This option is further enhanced by the increasing development of Virtual Reality Modelling Language (VRML), which allows virtual environments to be accessed over the web.

VRML

VRML is a computer language which describes a virtual space and makes it readable via a web-browser, usually in conjunction with a plug-in. Similar in principle to HTML (see Section 8.2), which describes document elements, VRML describes elements such as 'light source' and material types, which construct a 'virtual' environment. An example of VRML is as follows:

```
Collision {
collide TRUE
children [
PointLight {
intensity .5
location 23 14 -22
},
PointLight {
intensity 1
location 23 74 -22
},
Transform {
rotation – 1 0 0 1.57069
children [
Transform {
scale 46 44 1
children [
DEF aWall Shape {
appearance DEF wallMatl Appearance {
material Material {
ambientIntensity 0.13
diffuseColor 0.24 0.18 0.12
shininess 0.001
}
```

```
      }
      geometry DEF unitSquare rect { }
      }
    ]
    },
```

As can be seen from this example, the files created using VRML are *pure text*. This means that it is easy to transfer the file from one place to another. No specialist equipment is needed to create files like this, simply a knowledge of the language to create the environment.

In order to view the space a special viewer or browser is needed to interpret the language. A VRML viewer is usually a 'plug-in', which works in conjunction with a web browser. There are a number of different viewers and browsers which can be downloaded from various Internet sites.

VRML in the visual arts

As described above, VRML is being used in many different ways in the visual arts. It can be used to create an impression of a building, an interior of a building, or a three-dimensional model of a sculpture etc., or an interface to information resources.

An art-historical/cultural heritage orientated use of VRML is the re-creation of a chapel in Arezzo, Italy, painted by Piero della Francesca, a 15th-century fresco painter. The chapel was reproduced in a computer environment to be viewed in 3–D, and the viewer can move in all directions around the model to view the frescos. This example show how VR can be used successfully as a stimulating and dynamic interface for visual arts resources.

Another more recent example of a purely information interface is the VRML library catalogue of The Médiathèque. This is the multimedia library affiliated with the Institut de Recherche et Coordination Acoustique/Musique (IRCAM), Centre Georges Pompidou, Paris, France, available at: http://mediatheque.ircam.fr/index-e.html

Learning VRML

The VRML Repository (http://www.web3d.org/vrml/vrml.htm) is a good starting point to find out a bit more about browsers, with concise information about the different versions and their capabilities. This also gives links to a number of sites where both viewers and browsers are available.

An on-line tutorial for VRML is available through the Networked Virtual Reality Centre for Art and Design (NVRCAD): http://nvrcad.coventry.ac.uk

NVRCAD are also collaborating with VADS on a cross-disciplinary Arts and *Humanities Guide to Good Practice in Creating and Using Virtual Reality*.

8.4 COMPUTER AIDED DESIGN (CAD)

Introduction

CAD is software which can design in two and/or three dimensions, either by clicking with a mouse or entering co-ordinates via a keyboard. A mouse, or keyboard, is also used to move the user around the computer design.

The big difference between drawing on a computer and a drawing board is *scale*. With CAD, the object is drawn once, putting in lengths and widths by typing in the measurements. The scale is only important when printing or plotting a drawing or model.

CAD files utilise vector graphics, although raster images can be employed for rendering surfaces etc.

CAD also allows 'layers' to be used on a drawing or model. This means that a drawing can contain all the information about a building, for instance, but that it is possible to be selective about what is printed/outputted.

CAD systems include:

- AutoCAD
  (http://www.autodesk.com/products/acad2000/)
- ArchiCAD
  (http://www.graphisoft.com/)
- MiniCAD
  (http://www.diehlgraphsoft.com/support/minicad/minicad.html)

Good CAD systems should allow the design of buildings, models or objects with architecturally realistic 'ray tracing' and lighting models, or even animated fly-through or walk-through sequences.

CAD packages come with an increasing amount of 'production management' tools, making it possible to link the design and production processes through Computer Aided Manufacturing (CAM) packages and project management software.

CAD system costs

Prices can range from below £100 to thousands. When selecting a CAD package, it is important to consider the following needs

- Does it need to fit in with an existing system or client's system?
- Does it need to be able to draw three-dimensional objects?
- What are the number of users, their current training, etc?
- Hardware requirements
- Peripheral devices, for input and output

Hardware requirements

For serious CAD work the best of everything is required: optimum RAM and hard disk space, coupled with a fast graphics card and a high specification monitor.

Peripheral devices
These can include:

- A digitisation tablet to input data

- A plotter for output, although most applications will allow printing on A4 sheets
- A scanner to scan existing plans or images into a CAD system

CAD and the visual arts

CAD's main application within the visual arts will be for technical rather than information purposes, although CAD files themselves will become important archive documents. Thus CAD is mostly employed to design architecture or applied arts products. However, these increasingly powerful tools are capable of performing comparison and analysis of objects, and can be used in conjunction with on-site data recording devices to allow conservation analysis of buildings etc. over time.

8.5 INTERACTIVE MULTIMEDIA

Interactive multimedia, as the name implies, is a format where many media come together to complement one another. Thus text, sound, video, animation etc. can be combined, with each adding a different dimension to the resulting resource. One example of this is interactive encyclopaedias, e.g. Microsoft Encarta: http://www.encarta.msn.com/. Such encyclopaedias not only give information on a text and images basis, as paper encyclopaedias do, but they can also provide video, for instance, historical events, and animations, so allowing the user to interact with, e.g., demonstrations of the laws of perspective.

This combination of media can be very appealing and practical to the end-user, bringing added life and 'vibrancy' to a subject. One of the most prominent uses for multimedia in the visual arts is in the museum and art gallery environment. Institutions are installing terminals to inform the public of their collections. Two prominent examples of multimedia applications have been produced at the National Gallery (http://www.nationalgallery.org.uk/) and the Victoria and Albert Museum (http://www.vam.ac.uk/), both in London.

The National Gallery MicroGallery

This is a computerised information system of the National Gallery Collection enabling visitors to explore individual areas of interest, whether it be a particular painting, artist, period or subject matter. The MicroGallery can give a piece of text about a specific painting, along with a digital image of it, and allow sound to help the user pronounce artists' names etc. The user can also create their own gallery itinerary, as well as investigating detailed aspects of the works.

V&A Story of Glass

The V&A, when redeveloping their Glass Gallery, decided to install a multimedia installation which looked at the development of glass and its uses. The *Story of Glass* installation uses text, pictures, and video to describe the history of glass making and the designing processes.

Both MicroGallery and The Story of Glass enhance the visit to the respective institutions as they allow the visitor a more in-depth knowledge of the collections than perhaps was otherwise possible.

Multimedia resources are created using 'authoring' tools. These include:

- Asymmetric ToolBook (for the PC)
  http://www.asymetrix.com/products/
- IncWell Digital Media Group's SuperCard (for the Mac)
  http://www.incwell.com/SuperCard/SuperCard.html
- Macromedia Director (cross-platform).
  http://www.macromedia.com/software/director/

Such packages allow the author of the resource to combine images, text, sound and movie files within the software and then manipulate them as desired. A series of 'pages' or cells can be created and 'clickable' areas inserted into them to allow for movement through a resource or operation of an animation etc.

Although no specialist hardware is needed to create multimedia resources, the author of the resource will have to learn how to command the software to create the effects desired. Many of these authoring products have their own scripting language; for example Macromedia have developed 'Lingo' for their authoring product Director. Scripting languages will have to be learnt in order to use the full potential of the software. Multimedia authoring packages are also available either specifically for, or to be tailored to, web-authoring.

Whilst multimedia can be used as a strong presentation/publicity tool for digital resources, perhaps its strongest application within the visual arts is for Computer Assisted Learning (CAL), either for purely academic institutions or the educational missions of cultural heritage and other organisations.

8.6 DIGITAL ANIMATION

Using computers to aid the creation of animation is becoming more and more commonplace. Computers can aid in a variety of ways, from creating simple stills to complex morphing and distortion.

There are three primary types of computer animation:

- Rendering
- Cell animation
- Transition

Rendering

This relates to applying a surface to a digital object. Rendering requires a computer to use data, which includes structure and surface information, to create an object. The data will contain the information about what shapes are wanted and, using this information, the software can create a 'mesh' or 'wire-frame' showing the outlines of the objects required in the image. Once the 'mesh' has been created, images can then be rendered onto its surface.

This means that the image can be 'filled in', thus allowing colouring, shading, and the effect an object can have on an adjacent object. The ability to apply different textures is also possible, allowing for more realistic objects to be created.

Aspects to consider when rendering include:

- Colour theory
- Colour and light effects
- Reflection
- Transparency

All these play an important role when creating animation through rendering.

An example of rendering can be found at: http://www.bergen.org/AAST/ComputerAnimation/ Graph_Rendering.html

Cell animation

This is similar to traditional animation techniques. The animator can create single frames using a standard computer graphics tool, e.g. Photoshop, and then composite them. These can then be saved as a movie file or output to video. The introduction of computers to this way of creating animation has facilitated the process of creating both 'cells' and the animation 'reels'.

Transition

This is a way of moving from one image to another, for example fading where one image fades out and the next fades in. Other examples of transition include blending and morphing. Morphing is when two images appear to diffuse into one another in a flowing motion. Warping is the same as morphing, although a single image is distorted and no fade occurs. For further information on morphing, see: http://www.bergen.org/AAST/ComputerAnimation/Graph_Morphing.html

All the above effects are easily created when using a specialist animation software package which helps you create digital animation. For more information about the software and hardware which will aid the production of computer animation, please see the Computer Graphics and Animations Home Page

(http://www.bergen.org/AAST/ComputerAnimation/)

and specifically their section on Tools

(http://www.bergen.org/AAST/ComputerAnimation/CompAn_Tools.html)

Animation in web documents

Animation can be achieved in web documents through a variety of methods, including:

- Animated GIF
- Software created 'movies'

Animated GIF

An animated GIF is a graphic image on a Web page that changes and can therefore appear to move. For example, a twirling icon or a banner with a hand that waves or letters that increase in size. In particular, an animated GIF is a file in the Graphics Interchange Format (.GIF) that contains within the single file a set of images that are presented in a specified order. An animated GIF can loop endlessly, or it can present one or a few sequences and then stop the animation.

Software created 'movies'

JAVA, Shockwave, and other software tools can be used to build applets that achieve similar and other effects to an animated GIF. However, these require browsers and operating systems capable of handling such applets.

Animated GIFs can be handled by most browsers and are simpler to build than comparable images with Java or Shockwave.

Animation can certainly enhance digital resources created for the visual arts, especially in their visual appeal and level of interactivity. However, use of specialised packages may require extra skills to be learnt or brought on board.

Section 9: Conclusion: From Creation to Deposit – Working with VADS and TASI

9.1 ADVICE, CONSULTATION AND OUTREACH

Both the *Visual Arts Data Service* and the *Technical Advisory Service for Images* offer free services to members of the higher education community who are planning the creation of digital resources. While charges may be levied to organisations outside this community, and consultancy for commercial organisations may be arranged, neither VADS nor TASI charge for an *initial* consultation concerning digital resource creation or development. The reasoning behind VADS and TASI's work is to ensure that high quality digital resources are created which will inform and inspire educational excellence, whether they originate from within or outside UK H.E.

The services we are offering correspond to the diagrammatic framework in Figure 6, which indicates how the whole process of creating, managing and delivering a digital resource is inter-linked. Furthermore decisions about one aspect of the process directly influence the nature of another, so it is important to bear in mind the whole life-cycle of a digital project when planning to originate a new resource. For example, decisions about capture and creation will in the end affect data access and delivery. (See Section 5.1, for a description of the life-cycle of a digital resource.)

TASI offer advice on all aspects of the digitisation process for digital images, while VADS offers specific advice relating to the creation and use of digital resources in the visual arts subject area and also archiving, on-line delivery and digital preservation services for resources created by third parties. As a high proportion of the new digital resources that are being created in the visual arts community involve the generation of digital images, VADS and TASI have worked closely together to adopt a common framework for their advisory work, publications (of which this Guide is an example) and training events.

If after reading this Guide you require specific advice or training about the aspects of data creation and management covered within it, then this is available from VADS and TASI (see 'Who should I contact' below for an explanation of the nature of the advice provided by each organisation). Advice pertains to the following areas – which are linked to their relevant entry in this Guide.

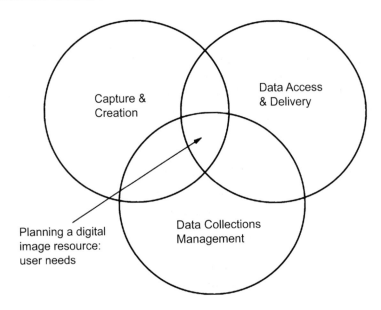

Figure 6: Resource creation phases

Data capture and creation

- Image handling, preparation: Section 3.7
- Image capture and manipulation: Sections 3.5, 3.6, 3.7
- Choosing file formats and compression: Section 3.3
- Copyright: Section 2.
- Data documentation and metadata: Section 4.

Data collections management

- Project management: Section 5.1
- Workflow and procedures management: Section 5.2
- Quality Assurance: Section 5.3
- Database creation and system design: Section 5.4

Advice on these areas is available to users through the following methods.

- One-to-one consultation
- Publications and on-line training materials
- Training events and workshops

Who should I contact?

If you are a member of the visual arts community who is interested in creating, using, or managing digital resources we recommend you contact VADS.

If your enquiry relates specifically to the creation and management of digital images, especially the technical aspects of this process, contact TASI. TASI's information is *not* subject specific.

See Appendix 1 for contact details

SECTION 9.2 DELIVERY, ACCESS, AND PRESERVATION

Once your resource has been created VADS and TASI can also offer you further assistance in the following areas, which also relates to areas covered in the Guide.

- Search and retrieval: Sections 6.2, 6.4
- User issues: Section 6.5
- Access management: Sections 6.3, 6.4
- Digital preservation: storage and archiving Section 7

VADS on-line resource delivery and preservation services

Furthermore, the remit of the Visual Arts Data Service is to provide an archiving service for digital resources of interest to the visual arts community for learning, teaching and research purposes. Archiving a digital resource involves two key activities.

- Firstly: developing an interface to the digital resource so it can be accessed on-line via the web.
- Secondly: storing and preserving resources so they are refreshed and migrated as technology moves on.

We recommend that you deposit with VADS whether or not you are storing and delivering your resource personally/locally. Resources in VADS archive contribute to a critical mass of materials whose contents can be cross-searched, therefore allowing new insights to be gained from deposited materials and the boundaries of the visual arts discipline(s) to be opened up and explored.

It is also the case that, as has been explained in Section 7., the preservation of digital materials is a complex, time consuming and costly process and one which it is often more appropriate to out-source to a dedicated service. Further information about the process of depositing with VADS is available on-line at http://vads.ahds.ac.uk

Appendix 1: VADS/TASI Contact details

Visual Arts Data Service:

VADS Office
Surrey Institute of Art & Design, University College
Falkner Road
Farnham
Surrey
GU9 7DS
Tel. +44 (0)1252 892723 / 4
Fax +44 (0)1252 892725
e-mail. info@vads.ahds.ac.uk
url: http://vads.ahds.ac.uk

Technical Advisory Service for Images:

TASI
Institute for Learning and Research Technology
University of Bristol
8–10 Berkeley Square
Bristol
BS8 1HH
Tel: 0117 928 7060
Fax: 0117 928 7112
e-mail. Info@tasi.ac.uk
url: http://www.tasi.ac.uk

Other useful organisations

The following projects and organisations are of relevance to the creation, development and use of digital resources within the visual arts. All these services are active at the time of publication:

AHDS

VADS is one of the five service providers of the Arts and Humanities Data Service. The service has four other branches and a Managing Executive which provide archiving and advisory services for archaeology, history, literature, and performing arts. All services can be reached through,
(http://ahds.ac.uk)

ADAM

The Art, Design, Architecture and Media Information Gateway is a service to help you find useful, quality-assured, information on the Internet in the following subject areas: art design, architecture and media. http://adam.ac.uk/

ADC–LTSN

LTSN Subject Centre for Art, Design and Communication is part of the new Learning and Teaching Support Network (LTSN) which comprises 24 Subject Centres, representing a wide range of subject areas in Higher Education. http://www.bton.ac.uk/adc-ltsn/

CHArt

Computers and the History of Art is a society open to all who have an interest in the application of computers to the study of art and design Chart publishes a refereed journal, and organises an annual conference. http://www.hart.bbk.ac.uk/chart

EDINA

EDINA is the JISC-funded national data centre which offers access to a library of data, information and research resources. Resources include HW Wilson's Art Abstracts and Palmer's Index to the Times. http://edina.ed.ac.uk/index.shtml

HEDS

HEDS is a JISC Service run by the University of Hertfordshire to provide a range of services to support the conversion of high volumes of teaching, learning and scholarly materials from paper and other formats to electronic form. The Digitisation Service focuses on expert advice and consultancy, with a total management package to provide complete digitisation services from feasibility assessment to final product delivery. Whilst HEDS is aimed at providing very low-cost services to the HE sector, it provides services at commercial rates for other clients as well. http://heds.herts.ac.uk

MDA

The MDA (Museum Documentation Association) is the lead body in the UK for museum information management and is supported in its work by the Museums and Galleries Commission, the Council of Museums in Wales, The Department of Education in Northern Ireland and the Scottish Office Education Department. http://www.mda.org.uk/

NETSKILLS

Netskills helps the UK higher education community develop the network skills to make effective use of the Internet for teaching, research and administration. http://www.netskills.ac.uk/

NVRCAD

The Networked Virtual Reality Resource Centres for Art and Design (NVRCADs) aim to provide a service to the art and design sector of higher education which should enable staff and students to gain greater access to digital three-dimensional environments.
http://vr3.tees.ac.uk/rachael/#prospectus

NPO

The National Preservation Office provides an information service and advocates best practice in preservation and security.
http://minos.bl.uk/index.html

TLTSN

Teaching and Learning Technology Support Network offers advice and guidance on the use of learning technology.
http://www.tltp.ac.uk/tltsn/

Appendix 2

PRIMARY IMAGE CAPTURE WORKFLOW DIAGRAM, SECTION 3.7

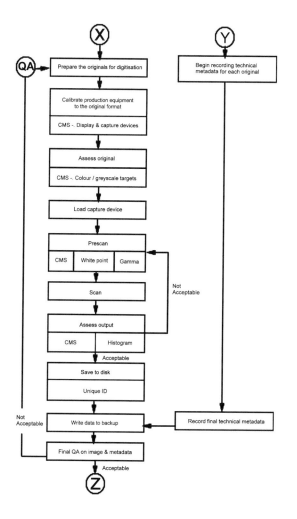

Figure 7: Primary Image capture workflow diagram

Adapted with kind permission from HEDS/TASI.
For the unedited JIDI workflow report see: http://www.tasi.ac.uk/building/workflow1.html
For the full JIDI Feasibility Study report see: http://heds.herts.ac.uk/Guidance/JIDI_fs.html

Appendix 3

 Visual **A**rts **D**ata **S**ervice

VADS Case Studies

An integral part of the work of the Visual Arts Data Service is identifying examples of current practice from projects involved with the digitisation of visual art material. These case studies will be a key source of evidence on which to base our guidelines for recommended practice. It is also apparent that it will only be possible to make practical recommendations to the community that are based on the experience of recent data creators, calling on what can be learnt from their achievements and also from the problems they have experienced.

Glossary

B

Backward compatibility
The ability for a computer application to read files which were created in a previous version of the software. A computer is said to be backward compatible if it can run the same software as the previous model of the computer.

C

CAD
Computer Aided Design. Software that utilises vector graphics to design in two and three dimensions.

CD-ROM
In computers, CD-ROM technology is a format and system for recording, storing, and retrieving electronic information on a compact disk that is read using an optical drive. It holds up to 600 megabytes of information.

Colour swatches
A sample set of a colour palette.

Calibration targets
Standard colour or greyscale charts from which image capture device specifications can be determined and accounted for.

Charged Couple Device
An electronic light sensing device.

D

DAT (Digital Audio Tape)
A helical-scan recording method initially developed to record CD-quality sounds on high-density audio tapes. It was quickly adapted for data storage applications. While DAT cartridges are all the same size (2.1 by 2.9 by 0.4 inches), the properties of the tape inside them differ. The smaller-capacity drives use tape cartridges that can store 1.3GB to 2GB of uncompressed data, and they have typical transfer rates ranging from 183KB per second (KBps) to 366KBps.

Their larger-capacity siblings support tape cartridges that store anywhere from 3GB to 4GB of uncompressed data, with typical transfer rates ranging from 366KBps to 510KBps. Many DAT drives offer some type of hardware-based data compression, which can significantly increase capacities and decrease transfer rates, depending on the type of data being stored.

Database
A generic term commonly used to describe a structured collection of data. Databases can take many forms including unstructured full text, images, maps, statistics or a mixture of data sources.

Data model
The theoretical model by which data are structured. Common data models include relational, network, hierarchical and object-oriented. Data modelling is a methodology for structuring data for use in database system.

Densitometers
A measuring device that registers the density of reflective or transparent materials.

DLT (Digital Linear Tape)
Digital Linear Tape Drive (DLT) provides a very fast (800 Kbytes per second) backup to tape cartridges that hold either 20 gigabytes or 40 gigabytes of data and can be mounted in an automated library that holds enough cartridges to backup 5.2 terabytes of data

Dublin Core
A 15 field standard for metadata – or 'electronic information about electronic information'. Full details are available from: http://www.purl.oclc.org/metadata/dublin_core

DVD (Digital Versatile Disc)
This is an optical disk technology that is expected to replace the CD-ROM disk rapidly (as well as the audio compact disc) over the next few years. The digital versatile disk (DVD) holds 4.7 gigabytes of information on one of its two sides, or enough for a 133–minute movie. With two layers on each of its two sides, it will hold up to 17 gigabytes of video, audio, or other information.

E

Encryption
The conversion of data into a form, called a cipher, that secures against unauthorised access to data.

EPS
Encapsulated PostScript. An image-storage format that extends the PostScript page-description language to include images.

F

FireWire (P1394)

This is an IEEE-standard hot pluggable serial bus. FireWire offers data trasfer speeds of up to 100 Mbps.

FTP

File Transfer Protocol. A common method for transferring files across the Internet.

Floppy Disk

The standard 3.5 inch portable computer disk, able to hold up to 1.4MB of data.

G

Gamma

The tonal range of an image.

Greyscale

The range of shades of grey in an image. The grey scales of scanners and terminals are determined by the number of greys, or steps between black and white, that they can recognise and reproduce.

GIF

Graphics Interchange Format. A bitmap graphics format from CompuServe which stores screen images economically and aims to maintain their correct colours even when transferred between different computers. GIF files are limited to 256 colours and like TIFFs, they use a lossless compression format but without requiring as much storage space.

H

Hardware

The physical components of computer systems, the hard disk, monitor etc, and peripheries such as mouse, keyboard, scanner.

I

ICC profiles

International Color Consortium colour standards. For further information see: http://www.color.org

Intranet

A 'private' computer network, accessible only to particular persons, usually within a distinct organisation or institution. (As opposed to the Internet, which is a publicly accessible network.)

IP

Internet Protocol – one of the main protocols behind the working of the Internet. It is the method by which data is sent between computers on the Internet.

ISO film speed

The standard for quoting photographic film speeds. It relates to the film's reactivity to light.

Interoperability

The ability of disparate computer systems to exchange information with one another, especially databases.

J

JAVA

A programming language which is platform independent, thus allowing the applications it creates (known as applets) to be run on any machine.

JAZ

A small, portable disk drive, developed by Iomega Corporation. Each JAZ drive disk holds 2GB.

JPEG

(Joint Photographic Experts Group), A digital image file format designed for maximal image compression. JPEG uses "lossy" compression in such a way that, when the image is decompressed, the human eye won't find the loss too obvious. The amount of compression is variable and the extent to which an image may be compressed without too much degradation depends partly on the image and partly on its use.

L

Landscape

This refers to the orientation of an image. Landscape describes an image which is wider than it is tall. (An image that is taller than it is wide is referred to as 'portrait'.)

Lossless compression

These compression formats, such as those used in GIF and TIFF files, retain all of the image data.

Lossy compression

Lossy compression algorithms compress the image file by removing image details – usually the details that the eye does not perceive very well to start with.

LS120

This is a 'super' floppy disk system, with the disks capable of storing up to 120MB.

Lux
A unit of illumination (one lumen per square metre).

M

Metadata
Electronic information about electronic information. The additional information used to describe something for a particular purpose (although that may not preclude its use for multiple purposes).

N

Non-proprietary
Material, (particularly software), that is not subject to ownership and control.

O

On-the-fly
Computer operations that develop or occur dynamically in 'real-time', rather than as the result of something that is statically predefined.

Open systems architecture
An architecture whose specifications are public. This includes officially approved standards as well as privately designed architectures whose specifications are made public by designers.

Operational specification
A definition of working parameters.

Optical Disk
Storage media that are based on optical rather than magnetic technologies, e.g. CD-ROMs, DVDs etc, where a laser reads 'pits' in the recorded surface of the disk.

P

Phosphors
These are materials that illuminate when struck by electrons. They produce the images on monitor screens. There are three different phosphors used, Red, Green, and Blue.

Photo-realistic
Representing an object 'as is', that is without any optical 'effects' etc. having been added.

Platform
A term that defines both the operating system of the computer and its hardware base, usually referring to the central processing unit.

Platform independent
Software or digital formats that can be used on any computer system regardless of the operating platform.

Plug-in
Plug-in applications are programs that can easily be installed and used as part of a Web browser, for example to view digital animations.

PNG
Portable Network Graphics. Pronounced 'ping' The PNG format is intended to provide a portable, legally unencumbered, well-compressed, well-specified standard for lossless raster/ bitmapped image files. Full details available from:
http://www.eps.mcgill.ca/~steeve/PNG/png.html

Portrait
This refers to the orientation of an image. Portrait describes an image which is taller than it is wide. (An image that is wider than it is tall is referred to as 'landscape'.)

PowerPoint
Microsoft's presentation software.

Proprietary
Material that is owned and controlled.

R
RAM
Random Access Memory – the part of a computer's memory where data is temporarily stored while being worked on.

Raster
A way of displaying spatial information as coloured grid cells. Also referred to as bitmap, as effectively a map of bits is evident.

Ray tracing
A technique for adding realism to computer models by including variations in shade, colour intensity, and shadows that would be produced by having one or more light sources. Ray tracing software simulates the path of light rays as they would be absorbed or reflected by objects.

Render
Adding realism to computer models, by for example applying a surface image to a geometrical frame.

S

Screen gamma values
The tonal specification for a computer screen.

Server
Computer that performs functions for other 'client' computers.

Software
Computer programs in machine readable form.

Specular
Bright reflection from a light source.

SPIFF/SPF
Still Picture Interchange File Format – this is the 'official' JPEG digital image format. As a relatively new format current support is low but this should change as the format has a lot to offer and has been designed so that most applications supporting JFIF/JPG should be able to read SPIFF files. Some of the supported features include: lossless and lossy compression (as SPF and JPG respectively); gamma; alternative colour spaces (e.g. RGB, CMY, PhotoYCC, video); text data fields (e.g. copyright, description, time/date etc.); thumbnails etc.

T

TFT panel
Thin Film Transistor display screen, such as a liquid crystal display (LCD) screen, common in notebook and laptop computers. Such screens have a transistor for each pixel (that is, for each of the tiny elements that control the illumination of the display). TFT is also known as active matrix technology in contrast to 'passive matrix' screens which do not have a transistor at each pixel.

Thumbnail
Low resolution digital images, usually used for quick reference and linkage to a larger higher quality image.

TIFF
Tagged Interchangeable File Format – TIF (PC) or TIFF (Macintosh). A widely used graphic image format, which is recommended for master copies and archival purposes.

True-colour
Usually refers to 24bit (or better) images.

U

UNIX
An operating system developed for workstations and client/server systems.

URL

Uniform Resource Locator. A standard addressing scheme used to locate or reference files on the Internet. Used in World Wide Web documents to locate other files. A URL gives the type of resource (scheme) being accessed (e.g. gopher, ftp) and the path to the file. The syntax used is: scheme://host.domain[:port]/path filename

V

VDU

Visual Display Unit – a computer monitor.

Vector

A geometric way of displaying spatial information as a series of points, lines and polygons.

W

Web Browser

A Web browser is a piece of software which allows access to the World Wide Web. It interprets HTML, displaying the data in an easy to read format. There are two distinct types of browser – graphical and non-graphical or text only. Typical graphical browsers are Netscape Navigator/Communicator and Microsoft Internet Explorer. An example of a text only browser is Lynx.

White-point

A definable reference point that indicates the lightest area of an image, causing all other areas to be adjusted in relation to it.

Z

Z39.50

A data protocol that allows disparate databases to communicate with each other.

ZIP

A small, portable disk drive; each Zip disk holds 100MB.

Selected Bibliography

Advisory Group on Computer Graphics, 1994. *The Use of I.T. in Art and Design*. Loughborough: AGOCG. (Part of the Technical Report Series/AGOCG; No.26).

Asmussen Interactive, 1999. *The Flash Guide*, [online]. Available from http://www.turtleshell.com/asm/tutorials/ [Accessed 09 Feb 2000]

Association of University Teachers, 1999. *Your Guide to Intellectual Property Rights*. London: AUT.

Baca, M., 1998. *Introduction to Metadata: Pathways to Digital Information*, [online]. Los Angeles: Library of Congress Cataloging-in-Publication Data, The Getty Information Institute, The Getty Center. Available from http://www.getty.edu/gri/standard/intrometadata/ [Accessed 08 Feb 2000]

Ball, S., Clark, S. and Windsor, P., 1998. The Care of Photographic Materials and Related Media: Guidelines on the Care. Handling, Storage and Display of Photography, Film, Magnetic and Digital Media. London: Museums and Galleries Commission.

Beagrie, N. and Greenstein, D., 1998. *A Strategic Policy Framework for Creating and Preserving Digital Collections*, [online]. Arts and Humanities Data Service Executive. Available from http://ahds.ac.uk/manage/framework.htm [Accessed 08 Feb 2000]

Beagrie, N. and Greenstein, D., 1998. *Managing Digital Collections: AHDS Policies, Standards and Practices*, [online]. Arts and Humanities Data Service. Available from http://ahds.ac.uk/public/srg.html [Accessed 08 Feb 2000]

Bearman, D., 1999. *NISO/CLIR/RLG Technical Metadata Elements for Images Workshop,* held: April18 and 19, 1999, Washington, DC. [online]. Bethesda: National Information Standards Organization (NISO). Available from http://www.niso.org/image.html [Accessed 08 Feb 2000]

Bearman, D., 1999. Reality and chimeras in the preservation of electronic records. *D-Lib Magazine* [online], 5 (4), January 2000, Corporation for National Research Initiatives: Digital Libraries Initiative. Available from http://www.dlib.org/dlib/april99/bearman/04bearman.html [Accessed 08 Feb 2000]

Berkeley Digital Library. *Imaging Information*, [online]. Available from http://sunsite.berkeley.edu/Imaging/ [Accessed 08 Feb 2000]

Besser, H. and Trant, J., 1995. *Introduction to Imaging*, [online]. Los Angeles: The Getty Information Institute, The Getty Center. Available from http://www.getty.edu/gri/standard/introimages/index.html [Accessed 08 Feb 2000]

Besser, H. and Yamashita, R., 1998. *The Cost of Digital Image Distribution: The Social and Economic Implications of the Production, Distribution and Usage of Image Data*, [online]. Berkeley: School of Information Management & Systems, UC. Available from http://sunsite.berkeley.edu/Imaging/Databases/1998mellon/ [Accessed 08 Feb 2000]

Besser, H., 1997. *Procedures and Practices for Scanning*, [online]. Canadian Heritage Information Network. Available from http://sunsite.Berkeley.EDU/Imaging/Databases/Scanning/ [Accessed 08 Feb 2000]

Besser, H., 1999. The MESL experience versus slide libraries: comparison and analysis. *Visual Resources*, 14 (4), 481–503.

Bide, M., Oppenheim, C. and Ramsden, A., 1997. *Copyright clearance and digitisation in UK Higher Education: Supporting Study for the JISC/PA Clearance Mechanisms Working Party*, [online]. Bath: UKOLN. Available from http://www.ukoln.ac.uk/services/elib/papers/pa/clearance [Accessed 03 Sept 1999]

Brennan, P., Hersey, K. and Harper, G., 1997. *Licensing Electronic Resources: Strategic and Practical Considerations for Signing Electronic Information Delivery Agreements*. Washington DC: Association of Research Libraries.

Campione, M. and Walrath, K., 1998. *The Java Tutorial: A Practical Guide for Programmers* [online]. Palo Alto, California: Sun Microsystems. Available from http://java.sun.com/docs/books/tutorial/ [Accessed 09 Feb 2000]

Carey, R. and Bell, G., 1997. *The Annotated VRML 2.0 Reference Manual*. Reading, Mass; Harlow: Addison-Wesley developers Press.

Cartwright, S and Gale, A., 1996. *Effective Teamworking in the Project Management Environment: Nurturing Diversity and Co-operation*. Eastham: Tudor.

Centre de Recherche en Droit Public (CRDP), 1995. *Crown Copyright in Cyberspace Conference*, [online]. Canada: University of Montreal. Available from http://www.droit.umontreal.ca/crdp/en/equipes/technologie/conferences/dac/index.html [Accessed 08 Feb 2000]

Cobley, A., 1997. *The Complete Guide to JAVA*. Southam: Computer Step.

Copyright Licensing Agency, [online]. Available from http://www.cla.co.uk/ [Accessed 03 Sept 1999]

Cornish, G. P., 1999. *Interpreting the Law for Libraries, Archives and Information Services*. 3rd edn. London: Library Association Publishing.

Council on Library and Information Resources. *CLIR Issues Newsletter* [online]. Washington: CLIR. Available from http://www.clir.org/pubs/issues/issues.html [Accessed 08 Feb 2000]

Council on Library and Information Resources. *Preservation and Access Newsletter* [online]. Washington: CLIR. Available from http://www.clir.org/pubs/pain/pain.html [Accessed 08 Feb 2000]

Davies, A., 1999. *The Digital Imaging A-Z*. Oxford: Focal Press.

Davis, P. T. and Lewis, B. D., 1996. *Computer Security for Dummies*. Foster City, CA: IDG Books Worldwide.

Day, M., 1998. *Metadata for Preservation: CEDAR Project Document AIW01*. Available from: http://www.ukoln.ac.uk/metadata/cedars/AIW01.html [Accessed 29 Sept 1999].

Day, M., 1999. Metadata for images: emerging practice and standards – *The Challenge of Image Retrieval: CIR 99 – Second UK Conference on Image Retrieval,* held 25–26 February 1999, Forte Posthouse Hotel, Newcastle upon Tyne, [online]. Bath: UKOLN, University of Bath. Available from http://www.ukoln.ac.uk/metadata/presentations/cir99/paper.html [Accessed 08 Feb 2000]

Dillon, A., 1996. *Myths, Misconceptions and an Alternative Perspective an Information Usage and the Electronic Medium*, [online] Indiana: School of Library and Information Science, Indiana University. Available from http://www.slis.indiana.edu/adillon/adillon-myths.html [Accessed 08 Feb 2000]

Dlm-Forum, 1998. *Guidelines on Best Practices for Using Electronic Information* [online] European Commission. Available from http://www2.echo.lu/dlm/en/gdlines.html [Accessed 08 Feb 2000]

Doucette, M., 1997. *Microsoft Project for Dummies*. Foster City, CA: IDG Books Worldwide.

Dublin Core Metadata Initiative. [Online]. Available from http://purl.org/dc/ [Accessed 03 Sept 1999]

Eakins, J. P. and Graham, M. E., 1999. *Content Based Image Retrieval: A Report to The JISC Technology Applications Programme.* Available from: http://www.unn.ac.uk/iidr/report.html [Accessed 29 Sept 1999]

Earnshaw, R. A., 1998. *Digital Media and Electronic Publishing.* London: Academic Press.

Eddy, S. E., 1997. *The GIF Animators Guide.* New York: MIS Press.

Eddy, S. E., 1998. *HTML in Plain English.* 2nd ed. New York: MIS Press.

Elkington, N., 1994. *Digital Imaging Technology for Preservation: Proceedings from an RLG Symposium* held March 17 and 18, 1994, *Cornell University, Ithaca, New York.* Mountain View, California: Research Libraries Group, Inc.

Ester, M., 1996. *Digital Image Collections: Issues and Practice.* Washington DC: Commission on Preservation and Access.

European Commision Legal Advisory Board, 1995.*The Information Society: copyright and multimedia*, [online]. Available from http://www2.echo.lu/legal/en/950426/toc.html [Accessed 08 Feb 2000]

Feeney, M (ed), 1999. *Digital Culture: Maximising the Nation's Investment: a synthesis of JISC/ NPO Studies on the Preservation of Electronic Materials.* London. The National Preservation Office.

Fleischhauer, C., 1998. Digital formats for content reproductions. *American Memory* [online]. Washington: Library of Congress. Available from http://memory.loc.gov/ammem/formats.html [Accessed 08 Feb 2000]

Fox, D. and Waite, M., 1984. *Computer Animation Primer.* New York; London: McGraw-Hill.

Getty Art History Information Program, 1994. *Authority Reference Tool: Users manual: Version 2 for the Art and Architecture Thesaurus.* 2nd ed. New York; Oxford: Oxford University Press.

Graham, I. S., 1998. *HTML Sourcebook.* New York; Chichester: Wiley.

Graham, M., 1999. *The Description and Indexing of Images: Report of a Survey of ARLIS Members, 1998/99.* Available from: http://www.unn.ac.uk/iidr/ARLIS/ [Accessed 29 Sept 1999]

Gray, S., 1998. *CAD/CAM in Clothing and Textiles.* Abingdon: Gower.

Greenstein, D. I., AND Miller, P., 1997. *Discovering On-line Resources Across the Humanities: A Practical Implementation of The Dublin Core.* Bath: UKOLN.

Hampson, A., 1999. *The Digital Imaging Handbook.* London: Library Association.

Hart, R.J and Baker and McKenzie, 1998. *Guide to Intellectual Property in the I.T. Industry.* London: Sweet and Maxwell.

Harvey, G., 1996. *Shockwave for Director 5 for Dummies.* Foster City, CA: IDG Books Worldwide.

Hedstrom, M., 1997. *Digital Preservation: A Time Bomb for Digital Libraries.* Computers and the Humanities, 31 (3) 189–201.

Hendley, T., 1998. *Comparison of Methods of Digital Preservation: A JISC/NPO Study of the Electronic Libraries (eLib), Programme on the Preservation of Electronic Materials.* London: Library Information Technology Centre. (Part of the Electronic Libraries Programme Studies series).

HMSO, 1988. *Copyright, Designs and Patents Act 1988.* London: HMSO.

Hodge, G. M., 2000. Best practices for digital archiving: an information life cycle approach. *D-Lib Magazine* [online], 6 (1), January 2000, Corporation for National Research Initiatives: Digital Libraries Initiative. Available from http://www.dlib.org/dlib/january00/01hodge.html [Accessed 08 Feb 2000]

Image Quality Working Group of Archives Com, 1997. *Technical Recommendations for Digital Imaging Projects,* [online]. New York: Joint Libraries/AcIS Committee, Columbia University. Available from http://www.columbia.edu/acis/dl/imagespec.html [Accessed 08 Feb 2000]

Instructional Technology Group. Animated GIFs. *ITG Web Design Tutorials,* [online]. Lincoln: University of Nebraska-Lincoln, Instructional Technology Group. Available from http://itg.unl.edu/teaching_resources/web_design_tutorials/animated/index.html [Accessed 09 Feb 2000]

Intellectual Property Right (IPR) Helpdesk, [online]. Available from http://www.cordis.lu/ipr-helpdesk/ [Accessed 08 Feb 2000]

Iuppa, N.V., 1998. *Designing Interactive Digital Media.* Oxford; Boston: Focal Press.

Joint Information Systems Committee, 1998. *JISC/TLTP Copyright Guidelines.* London: LITC

Joint RLG and NPO Preservation Conference, 1998. *Guidelines for Digital Imaging,* held 28 – 30 September 1998, Scarman House, The University of Warwick, [online]. Mountain View, California: Research Libraries Group, Inc. Available from http://lyra.rlg.org/preserv/joint confpapers.html [Accessed 08 Feb 2000]

Jones, M. L. W., Gay, G. K. and Rieger, R. H., Project soup: comparing evaluations of digital collection efforts. *D-Lib Magazine* [online], 5 (11), November 1999, Corporation for National Research Initiatives: Digital Libraries Initiative. Available from http://www.dlib.org/dlib/november99/11jones.html [Accessed 08 Feb 2000]

Keene, S., 1998. *Digital Collections: Museums and the Information Age.* Oxford; Boston: Butterworth-Heinemann.

Kenney, A. R. and Chapman, S. 1996. *Digital Imaging for Libraries and Archives.* Department of Preservation and Conservation, Cornell University Library.

Kling, R. and ELLIOTT, M., 1994. *Digital Library Design for Usability: Proceedings of the First Annual Conference on the Theory and Practice of Digital Libraries,* held 19–21 June, 1994, College Station, Texas. [online] College Station, Texas: Center for the Study of Digital Libraries. Available from http://www.csdl.tamu.edu/DL94/paper/kling.html [Accessed 08 Feb 2000]

Lander, R., 2000. *Generally Markup: XML Resources*, [online]. Available from http: pdbeam.uwaterloo.ca/~rlander/ [Accessed 09 Feb 2000]

Lee, S. L., 1997. Economics of digital information: collection, storage and delivery. *Journal of Library Administration*, 24 (4).

Lievesley, D. 1995. Strategies for managing electronic archives. *Long Term Preservation of Electronic Materials* [online] JISC, and The British Library. Available from: http://www.ukoln.ac.uk/services/papers/bl/rdr6238/ [Accessed 03 Sept 1999].

Loeb, L., 1998. *Secure Electronic Transactions: Introduction and Technical Reference.* Boston; London: Artech House. OPPLIGER, R., 1998. Internet and Internet Security. Boston; London: Artech House.

Machover, C., 1996. *The CAD/CAM Handbook.* New York: McGraw-Hill. (Part of the Visual Technology series).

Macromedia. *Dynamic HTML Zone.*[online]. Available from http://www.dhtmlzone.com/index.html [Accessed 09 Feb 2000]

Mealing, S., 1998. *The Art and Science of Computer Animation.* Oxford: Intellect Books.

National Center for Supercomputing Applications, 1999. *A Beginners Guide to HTML* [online] Champaign, Illinois: University of Illinois at Urbana-Champaign. Available from http://www.ncsa.uiuc.edu/General/Internet/WWW/HTMLPrimer.html [Accessed 09 Feb 2000]

National Science Foundation, 1999. *NSF Workshop Position Papers: NSF Workshop on Data Archival and Information Preservation,* held March 26–27, 1999, Washington DC, [online]. Missouri: College of Engineering. Available from http://cecssrv1.cecs.missouri.edu/ NSFWorkshop/NSFppapers.html [Accessed 08 Feb 2000]

O' Rourke, M., 1998. *Principles of Three-dimensional Computer Animation: Modelling, Rendering and Animating with 3D Computer Graphics*. New York; London: Norton.

Oppenheim, C., 1996. Legal issues associated with electronic copyright management systems. *Ariadne* [online], Issue 2. Bath: UKOLN. Available from http://www.ariadne.ac.uk/issue2/copyright/ [Accessed 03 Sept 1999]

Oppenheim, C., 1996. Moral rights and the electronic library. *Ariadne* [online], Issue 4. Bath: UKOLN. Available from http://www.ariadne.ac.uk/issue4/copyright/ [Accessed 03 Sept 1999]

Ostrow, S. E., 1998. *Digitizing Historical Pictorial Collections for the Internet*, [online]. Commission on Preservation and Access, Council on Library and Information Resources. Available from http://www.clir.org/pubs/reports/ostrow/pub71.html [Accessed 08 Feb 2000]

Paine, C., 1996. *Standards in the Museum Care of Photographic Collections*. London: Museums and Galleries Commission.

Pedley, P, 1998. *Copyright for Library and Information Service Professionals*. London: ASLIB (Part of the ASLIB Know How series).

Plant, D., 1998. *Flash!: Creative Web Animation*. Berkeley, CA: Macromedia Press.

Puglia, S., 1999. The costs of digital imaging projects. *RLG Diginews* [online], 3 (5), Oct 15 1999. Mountain View, California: Research Libraries Group, Inc. Available from http://www.rlg.ac.uk/preserv/diginews/diginews3–5.html [Accessed 08 Feb 2000]

Rebelsky, S. A. and Makedon, F., 1998. *Electronic Multimedia Publishing: Enabling Technologies and Authoring Issues*. Boston; London: Kluwer Academic. (A special issue of Multimedia Tools and Applications, An International Journal, 6 (2)).

Rohan, R. F., 1998. *Building Better Web Pages*. San Diego: AP Professional.

Ross, S., 1997. Preserving and maintaining electronic resources in the visual arts for the next century. *Computers and the History of Art*, 7 (2), 35–50.

Shiffman, H., 1998. *Making Sense of Java*, [online]. Mountain View, California: Disordered Thoughts. Available from http://www.disordered.org/Java-QA.html [Accessed 09 Feb 2000]

Smith, B and Bebak, A., 1998. *Creating Web Pages for Dummies*. 3rd ed. Foster City, CA: IDG Books Worldwide.

Smith, B., 1997. *AutoCAD 14.0 for Dummies*. 2nd ed. Foster City, CA: IDG Books Worldwide.

Steinhauer, L., 1996. *Macromedia Director 5 for Dummies*. 2nd ed. Foster City, CA: IDG Books Worldwide.

Stephenson, C. and McClung, P., (ed.) 1998. Delivering digital images: cultural heritage resources for education, *The Museum Educational Site Licensing Project, Volume 1* [online], Los Angeles: The Getty Center. Available from http://www.getty.edu/museum/mesl/reports/mesl_ddi_98/fm_ddi_001.html [Accessed 08 Feb 2000]

Sterling, J.A.L, 1999. *World Copyright Law: Protection of Authors Works, Performances, phonograms, films, video, broadcasts and published editions in National, International and Regional Law*. London: Sweet and Maxwell.

Stone, M., 1998. *VRML 2.0: Rendering Revealed* [online] VRML Color Fidelity Working Group. Available from http://www.parc.xerox.com/red/members/stone/vrml-cfwg/rendering/ [Accessed 08 Feb 2000]

Straten, Roelof van. 1994. *Iconography, Indexing, Iconclass: A Handbook*. Leiden: Foleor.

Sutcliffe, G., 1995. *Slide Collection Management in Libraries and Information Units*. Aldershot: Gower.

Tanner, S. and Lomax-Smith, J., 1999. Digitisation: how much does it really cost?. *Paper for Digital Resources for the Humanities 1999 Conference*. Available from http://heds.herts.ac.uk/HEDCinfo/Papers.html [Accessed 29 Sept 1999].

The International Federation of Library Associations and Institutions. *IFLA Electronic Collections*, [online]. Available from http://ifla.org/II/index.htm [Accessed 08 Feb 2000]

The National Preservation Office, 1998. *Guidelines for Digital Imaging:* Papers given at the Joint National Preservation Office and Research Libraries Group, Preservation Conference, held 28–30 Sept 1998, Warwick, UK. London: NPO.

The Task Force for the Archiving of Digital Information, 1996. *Preserving Digital Information* [online] California Commission for the Preservation of Access, and The Research Libraries Group. Available from: http://www.rlg.org/ArchTF [Accessed 30 July 1998].

Tittel (ed.), *Building VRML Worlds*. Berkeley, CA; London: Osborn/McGraw-Hill.

UKOLN, 1998. *Virtually New – Creating the Digital Collection: A Review of Digitisation Projects in Local Authorities, Libraries and Archives* [online]. Bath: Library and Information Commission Bath, UKOLN. Available from http://www.ukoln.ac.uk/services/lic/digitisation/ [Accessed 08 Feb 2000]

Vacca, J. R., 1997. VRML Clearly Explained. 2nd ed. Boston; London: AP Professional.

Visual Resources Association, 1997.*VRA Core Categories* [online]. Available from http://www.oberlin.edu/~art/vra/wc1.html [Accessed 08 Feb 2000]

VRML @ SIM [online]. Portugal: University of Minho, Department of Informatics. Available at http://sim.di.uminho.pt/vrml/ [Accessed 08 Feb 2000]

Wayner, P, 1997. *Digital Copyright Protection*. London and Boston, Mass: AP Professional.

Web Reference. *3D Animation Workshop* [online]. Internet.com Corporation. Available from http://www.webreference.com/3d/ [Accessed 09 Feb 2000]

Weber, H. and Dorr, M., 1997. *Digitization as a Means of Preservation?: European Commission on Preservation and Access,* Amsterdam, October 1997 [online] Washington: CLIR. Available from http://www.clir.org/pubs/reports/digpres/digpres.html [Accessed 08 Feb 2000]

Weibel, S. and Miller, E., 1997. Image description on the Internet: a summary of the CNI/OCLC image metadata workshop, held September 24 – 25, 1996, Dublin, Ohio. *D-Lib Magazine* [online], January 1997, Corporation for National Research Initiatives: Digital Libraries Initiative. Available from http://www.dlib.org/dlib/january97/oclc/01weibel.html [Accessed 08 Feb 2000]

Wilhelm, H., 1993. *The Permanence and Care of Color Photographs: Traditional and Digital Color Prints, Color Negatives, Slides and Motion Pictures*. Grinnell, Iowa: Preservation Pub. Co.

Williams, E. W., 1994. *The CD-ROM and Optical Recording Systems*. Oxford; New York: Oxford University Press.

Wired Digital Inc. *Webmonkey: The Web Developers Resource*, [online]. Lycos Network. Available from http://hotwired.lycos.com/webmonkey/multimedia/tutorials/tutorial1.html [Accessed 09 Feb 2000]

Wysocki, R.K., Crane, D.B. and Beck, R., 1995. *Effective Project Management: How to Plan Manage and Deliver On Time and Within Budget*. New York: Wiley.

XML Special Interest Group, 1999. *Frequently Asked Questions about the Extensible Markup Language*, [online]. World Wide Web Consortium (W3C). Available from http://www.ucc.ie/xml/ [Accessed 09 Feb 2000]

Youngs, K. J. and Brickely, D., 1998. *Metadata*. [Online]. Bristol: University of Bristol. Available from: http://www.tasi.ac.uk/building/metadata1.html [Accessed 03 September 1999].